Environmental Science

49 Science Fair Projects

Other Books in the
Science Fair Projects Series

BOTANY:

49 Science Fair Projects (No. 3277)

This first book in the series explores plant germination, photosynthesis, hydroponics, plant tropism, plant cells, seedless plants, and plant dispersal.

EARTH SCIENCE:

49 Science Fair Projects (No. 3287)

This second book in the series examines Earth's geology, meteorology, and oceanography, as well as the Earth's crust, weather, solar energy, acid rain, fossils, and rocks and minerals.

BOTANY:

49 More Science Fair Projects (No. 3416)

The tremendous interest and popularity of the first botany book commanded that another botany book be added to the series. Projects in plant germination, photosynthesis, hydroponics, plant tropism, plant cells, and plant dispersal, together with the first botany book, offer 98 complete projects with more than 200 ideas for going further.

Science Fair
Projects

Series

Environmental Science

49 Science Fair Projects

Robert L. Bonnet
G. Daniel Keen

TAB Books
Division of McGraw-Hill, Inc.
Blue Ridge Summit, PA 17294-0850

FIRST EDITION
SEVENTH PRINTING

Library of Congress Cataloging-in-Publication Data

Bonnet, Robert L.
    Environmental science : 49 science fair projects / by Robert L.
Bonnet and Daniel Keen.
        p.   cm.
    Summary: Suggests forty-nine projects in environmental science,
suitable for the classroom or a science fair.
    ISBN 0-8306-7369-5 — ISBN 0-8306-3369-3 (pbk.)
    1. Pollution—Experiments—Juvenile literature.   2. Ecology-
-Experiments—Juvenile literature.   3. Science projects—Juvenile
literature.   [1. Ecology—Experiments.   2. Experiments.   3. Science
projects.]   I. Keen, Dan.   II. Title.
TD178.B66   1990
628'.078—dc20   90-10905
                                              CIP
                                               AC

Acquisitions Editor: Kimberly Tabor
Book Editor: Lori Flaherty
Director of Production: Katherine G. Brown   SKF
Illustrations: Carol Chapin   3369

Contents

8 Man Affects the Environment   **97**

Projects in Mankind and the Environment

*To our parents: Olivia,
Robert, Amber, Martin, Doris,
Joe, George, and Marie.*

Acknowledgments

We wish to extend our appreciation to Tom Progranicy, Gary Patterson, Dr. Gene Vivian, John D. Webersinn, and W. Daniel Keen, R.P.

Introduction

At some time during our school years, all of us have been required to do at least one science project. It might have been growing seeds in kindergarten or building a Telsa coil in high school, but such experiences are not forgotten and help to shape our view of the world around us.

Doing a science project produces many benefits beyond the obvious educational value. The logical processes encourage clear, concise thinking, which can carry through a student's entire life. Science requires a discipline of the mind, clear notes and data gathering, curiosity, patience, an honesty about results and procedures, and last, a concise reporting of work accomplished. A successful science project might motivate a student to strive for success in other areas.

Many children discover a new spin-off interest by doing a science project. A child who does a mathematics project for a science fair, perhaps using batteries, switches, and light bulbs to represent binary numbers, might discover a liking for electronics. But where can students, teachers, or parents find suggestions for science projects?

The Science Fair Projects Series offers a large collection of science fair projects and project ideas. Teachers can use these books for classroom instruction, as a springboard for classroom projects, or even to suggest criteria for judging.

If you are a parent who wants to help your child with a science fair project but feel apprehensive, these books can come to your rescue. In fact, we encourage you to work with your children on science projects. Not only will you be enriching your family relationships, but you can enhance your child's self-esteem.

Finally, you might want to do some of these projects just for fun. If your science education was a little more than lacking, you'll not only have fun, you'll learn a few new things. No matter who you are, this book shows you project ideas from beginning to end.

Students need a starting point. They also need direction. That's why each project begins with an overview of the subject and some suggestions for a possible hypothesis. Each project also includes a materials list, procedures, data gathering and organizational direction, and controls. To encourage students to develop the ideas they learned using valid scientific processes, each project ends with several suggestions for taking the project further.

Chapters are organized by topics. Although some projects might overlap into more than one science discipline, we have attempted to place these projects under their dominant theme. You can quickly skim through the topics to find a project that is suitable for the ability of your group or that sparks your interest. Be sure to read the introduction at the beginning of each chapter, however. The information is relevant to the projects in that section. The Resource List at the back of the book lists suppliers where you can purchase laboratory supplies.

Projects are designed for sixth to ninth grade students. Many projects can be "watered down," however, and used for children in lower grades. Similarly, students in higher grades can use the additional ideas at the end of each project to achieve more advanced levels.

After you have selected a project and read the introduction, read the entire project through carefully. This will help you understand the overall scope of the project, the materials you need, the time requirements, and the procedures.

There is no limit to the number of themes and the number of hypotheses one can form about our universe. It is as infinite as the stars in the heavens. Hopefully, many students will be creative with the ideas presented, develop their own unique hypotheses, and proceed with their experiments using accepted scientific methods.

Some projects can go on for years. There is no reason to stop a project other than getting tired of it. It may be that what you studied this year can be taken a step further next year. With each question or curiosity answered, more questions are raised. It has been our experience that answers produce new and exciting questions. We believe that science discovery and advancement proceeds as much on excellent questions as it does on excellent answers.

We hope we can stimulate the imagination and encourage creative thinking in students, teachers, and parents. Learning is rewarding and enjoyable. Best of luck with your project.

Robert L. Bonnet
G. Daniel Keen

How to Use This Book

All projects that require adult supervision have the **STOP** symbol at the beginning of the project. No responsibility is implied or taken for anyone who sustains injuries as a result of the materials or ideas put forward in this book. Taste nothing that is not directly food related. Use proper equipment (gloves, safety glasses, and other safety equipment). Clean up broken glass with a dust pan and brush. Use chemicals with extra care. Wash hands after project work is done. Tie up loose hair and clothing. Follow step-by-step procedures; avoid shortcuts. Never work alone. Remember, adult supervision is advised. Use common sense and make safety the first consideration, and you will have a safe, fun, educational, and rewarding project.

1

Science Projects

$\mathbf{B}$efore you begin working on a science project, there are some important things you need to know. It is important that you read this chapter before starting on a project. It defines some of the terms used in this book and sets up guidelines that should be adhered to as work on the project progresses.

Beginning without Pain

Before you can do a science project, you must first fully understand the term *science project*. Older students are familiar with report writing. Many types of reports are required at all grade levels, whether it be book reports, history reports, or perhaps term papers. Although a report might be required to accompany a science project, it is not the focal point. The body of science comes from experimentation. Most projects discover information by scientific methods. The scientific method is a formal approach to scientific investigation. It is a step-by-step, logical thinking process and can be grouped into four sections:

1. The statement of the problem.

2. The hypothesis.

3. Experimentation and information gathering (results).

4. A conclusion based on the hypothesis.

In science, a statement of the "problem" does not necessarily mean that something went wrong. A problem is something for which there is no good answer. Air pollution is a problem. Aggressive behavior, crab grass, and obesity are problems. Any question can be stated as a problem.

Discuss your ideas with someone else, a friend, a teacher, a parent, or someone working in the field you are investigating. Find out what has already been done on the subject and if the scope of your project is appropriate.

A hypothesis is an educated guess. It is educated because you have knowledge about trees, dogs, or whatever the subject matter might be. Your life experiences help you form a specific hypothesis rather than a random one. Suppose you hypothesize, "If I add sugar to water, and feed it to this plant, it will grow better." A "control" plant would be needed, namely, a plant that was given only water. Both plants would be given the identical amount of sunshine, water, temperature, and any other nonexperimental factors.

Assumptions

Any assumption in science must be specifically defined. What is meant by saying "The plant will grow better?" What is "better" assumed to be? Does it mean greener leaves, faster growing, bigger foilage, better tasting fruit, more kernels per cob?

If you are growing plants from seeds, the assumption is made that all of the seeds are of equal quality. When several plants are used in an experiment, it is assumed that all the plants are the same at the start of the project.

Before beginning a project, be sure to state all your assumptions. If the results of an experiment are challenged, the challenge should be on the assumptions and not on the procedure.

Sample Size

"Sample size" refers to the number of items in a test. The larger the sample size, the more significant the results. Using only two plants to test the sugar theory would not yield a lot of confidence in the results. One plant might have grown better than the other because some plants just grow better than others. Obviously, our statistical data becomes more meaningful as we sample a larger group of items in the experiment. As the group size increases, individual differences have less importance.

Making accurate measurements is a must. The experimenter must report the truth, and not let bias (his or her feelings) affect his measurements. As we mentioned earlier, the reason science progresses is because we do not have to reinvent the wheel. Science knowledge builds on what people have proven before us. It is important to document (record) the results. They must be replicable (able to be repeated), so others can duplicate our efforts. Good controls, procedures, and clear recordkeeping are essential. As information is gathered, the results might lead to further investigation or raise more questions that need asking.

The conclusion must be related to the hypothesis. Was the hypothesis correct or incorrect? Perhaps it was correct in one aspect but not in another. In the sugar example, adding sugar to the water may have helped, but only to a point. The human body can use a certain amount of sugar for energy, but too much could cause obesity.

There is no failure in a science experiment. The hypothesis might be proven wrong, but learning has still taken place. Information has been gained. Many experiments prove to be of seemingly no value, except that someone reading the results will not have to spend the time repeating the same experiment. That is why it is important to thoroughly report results. Mankind's knowledge builds on success and failure.

Collections, Demonstrations, and Models

Competitive science fairs usually require experimentation. Collections and models by themselves are not experiments, although they can be turned into experiments. A collection is gathered data. Suppose a collection of shells has been assembled from along the eastern seaboard of the United States. The structure and composition of shells from the south can be compared to those found in the north. Then the collection becomes more experimental. Similarly, an insect collection can deal with insect physiology or comparative anatomy. A rock and mineral collection might indicate a greater supply of one type over another because of the geology of the area from which they were collected. Leaves could be gathered from trees to survey the available species of trees in your area.

Classroom assignments that use demonstrations or models can help students better understand scientific concepts. A steam engine dramatically shows how heat is converted to steam and steam is converted into mechanical energy. Seeing it happen might have greater educational impact than merely talking about it.

Individuals Versus Group Projects

A teacher might require a group of students to work on a project, but groups can be difficult for a teacher to evaluate. Who did the most work? If, however, it is being dealt with on an interest level, then the more help received, the better the project might be. Individual versus group projects bear directly on the intended goal. Keep in mind, however, that most science fairs do not accept group projects.

Choosing a Topic

Select a topic of interest; something that arouses curiosity. One only needs to look through a newspaper to find a contemporary topic: dolphins washing up on the beach, the effect of the ozone layer on plants, stream erosion, etc.

Limitations and Precautions

Of course, safety must always be placed first when doing a project. Using voltages higher than those found in batteries have the potential of electrical shock. Poisons, acids, and caustics must be carefully monitored by an adult. Temperature extremes, both hot and cold, can cause harm. Sharp objects or objects that can shatter, such as glass, can be dangerous. Nothing in chemistry should be tasted. Combinations of chemicals may produce toxic materials. Safety goggles, aprons, heat gloves, rubber gloves for caustics and acids, vented hoods, and adult supervision are just some safety considerations. Each project should be evaluated for the need of these various safety materials. Projects that require adult supervision have the (STOP) symbol at the beginning of the project. Finally, projects that will be left unattended and accessible to the public should be given special consideration.

Most science fairs have ethical rules and guidelines for live animals, especially vertebrates, that are given thoughtful consideration. In some cases, you could be required to present a note from a veterinarian or other professional that states the training the animal has received. One example, is to have mice run through a maze to demonstrate learning or behavior.

Limitations on time, help, and money are also important factors. How much money will be spent should be addressed by a science fair committee. Generally, when a project is entered in a science fair, the more money spent on the display, the better the chance of winning. It isn't fair that one child might only have $1.87 to spend on a project while another may have $250. Unfortunately, at many science fairs the packaging does influence the judging. An additional problem might be that one student's parent is a science teacher and another student's parent may be unavailable or unable to help.

Science Fair Judging

In general, science fairs lack well-defined standards. The criteria for evaluation can vary from school to school, area to area, and region to region. We would like to propose some goals for students and teachers to consider when judging.

A winning project should be one that requires creative thinking and investigation by the student. Recordkeeping, logical sequence, presentation, and originality are also important points.

The thoroughness of the student's project reflects the background work that was done. If the student is present, a judge could orally quiz to see if the experimenter has sufficient understanding. Logging all experiences, such as talking to someone knowledgeable in the subject or reading material on it, will show the amount of research put into the project. Consequently, urge students to keep a record of all the time they spend on a project.

Clarity of the problem, assumptions, procedures, observations, and conclusions are important judging criteria as well. Be specific.

Points should be given for skill. Skills could be in computation, laboratory work, observation, measurement, construction, and the like. Technical ability and workmanship are necessary to a good project.

Often, projects with flashier display boards do better. Some value should be placed on dramatic presentation, but it should not outweigh other important criteria, such as originality. Graphs, tables, and other illustrations can be good visual aids to the interpretation of data. Photographs are especially important for projects where it is impossible to set the project up indoors (a "fairy ring" of mushrooms in the forest, for example).

Some science fairs might require a short abstract or synopsis in logical sequence. It should include purpose, assumptions, a hypothesis, materials, procedure, and conclusion.

Competing

Often, a project will compete with others, whether it is at the class level or at a science fair. Find out ahead of time what the rules are for the competition. Check to see if there is a limit on project size. Will an accompanying research paper be required? Will it have to be orally defended? Will the exhibit have to be left unattended overnight? Leaving a $3,000 computer unattended overnight would be a big risk.

Find out which category has the greatest competition. You may be up against less competition by placing your project in another category. If it is a "crossover" project, you might want to place it in a category that has fewer entries. For example, a project that deals with chloroplasts could be classified under botany or under chemistry. A project dealing with the wavelength of light hitting a plant could be botany or physics.

Environmental Science

This book deals with a wide range of ideas in the category of environmental science. Environment is all around you, wherever you are, at home, at school, in your yard, inside a car (or bus), or swimming in a lake (or a pool). Air, water, food, and the materials found in them make up part of the environment.

The Earth's environment is a "closed system." All of the resources and products are here and stay here. We are a spaceship with everything we need on board. How we deal with this environment will affect people today and for generations to come. Therefore, the better we understand our environment, the better equipped we will be to utilize and protect it.

When people speak of "mother nature," the reference is really to the environment of the Earth. Nature is a balanced system. This balance is achieved in part because many things carry on in a cycle. Oxygen, water, nitrogen, and even rocks are in a cycle. Every natural catastrophe (flood, volcanic eruption, drought) is countered by some other occurrence. Forest fires allow for new young forests. Insect pests might cause crop problems, but could be an increased food supply for other organisms. Nature restores itself over a long period of time.

Man is within, and a part of, the environment. His ability to cause change, however, is much greater than that of all other organisms combined. It is this responsibility that mankind must acknowledge.

Projects in environmental science can evaluate the outcomes when organisms interact with nonliving materials and when organisms interact with other organisms. An example of an organism interacting with a nonliving material is a beaver damming up a stream. An example of organisms dealing with other organisms would be predator/prey relationships, such as an eagle eating a snake. Because of this interaction, we should take a world view of our activities. Planning our activities (especially as a society) should include evaluating the environmental impact 50 to 100 years from now, and not just for the short-term. A building developer might want to cut down trees to make a 5 million dollar profit today, but how will his action affect life 50 years from now? On a larger scale, will our actions cause the extinction of a plant or animal species? Should it be a goal to avoid extinction of animals and plants?

An excellent place to start studying the environment is wherever you find yourself right now. Many projects in this book take this basic, yet often overlooked approach.

Complete projects are shown under topic categories, which are listed as chapter titles. Many additional ideas for going further are brainstormed and are left for the reader to develop and investigate. Most of the equipment and supplies required for these projects are inexpensive items or items that can be found around the home. A Resource List gives supplies required for some projects.

A project should not require equipment or supplies beyond what can be obtained. For example, a project requiring lodgepole pine cones should not be attempted if these cones are not available.

2

Under Your Feet

The material located under your feet determines what can grow there, and what grows there will determine which animals will live there. The Panda of Asia needs bamboo. When stands of bamboo are cut down in order to develop housing, Pandas living in the area will be stressed for food. This means there will not be enough food for the Panda population. If the soil conditions do not support the growth of bamboo, animals that eat it (such as the Panda) must live elsewhere.

A "biome" is a classification of an area due to the conditions that exist in that area. Biomes have specific climates; deserts are hot and dry, rain forests are wet and humid, the polar caps are cold and dry. Another term "ecosystem" refers to both the living and nonliving things found in an area.

PROJECT 2-1
Homemade Topsoil
Adult Supervision Required

Overview

Topsoil contains particles of broken rock, decomposing organic material (called humus), living organisms, oxygen and other gases, minerals, moisture, and sometimes tin cans, bottles, and old bicycles! Topsoil supports the growing vegetation in many ways. It offers physical support to plants by anchoring root systems. It supplies moisture, minerals, and aeration, as well as keeping the roots at a more constant temperature than the surrounding air. The earth is creating topsoil all of the time. Hypothesize that you can duplicate nature by making your own topsoil. Can it be used to grow plants and vegetables? Be advised that this is a long-term project. It will take several months to complete.

Materials

- 2 quarts of small, local rocks (smaller than an egg)
- 12 quarts of leaves, twigs, and bark (mixed together)
- peels from several dozen citrus fruits (lemons, oranges, grapefruit)
- large tub (to mix it in)
- hammer
- burlap bag
- safety goggles

Procedure

Gather the materials. Rinse the rocks to remove any soil. Place the rocks in a burlap bag, put on safety glasses, and pulverize them with a hammer. Break the rocks down until all of the pieces are smaller than a pea. Place them in a large tub. Pour the rock dust particles in too. Add 12 quarts of leaves, twigs, and bark. Add the peels from several dozen citrus fruits (their acid will help break down the other materials. Pour enough water into the mixture to completely cover all of the ingredients. Let it stand for several months, stirring the mixture every week. Add water when needed to maintain a cover over the materials.

After several months, let the water evaporate. Mix thoroughly. Use the homemade topsoil as potting soil and attempt to grow plants and vegetables. Observe and record data as the plants grow. Was your hypothesis correct or incorrect?

Going Further

Use old tea bags (tannic acid), including the string and tab, to help break down materials.

PROJECT 2-2
A Slice of Life

Overview

Areas of land are often named after the largest dominant plant species found in that area, such as the New Jersey pine barrens and cedar forests (Fig. 2-1). Topsoil in one area might be thicker (or thinner) than in another. Do certain tree and plant species grow in an area because the topsoil is at the thickness they need or is the topsoil as thick as it is because of the litter (decomposing leaves, twigs, branches) falling from the trees? Hypothesize what the thickness of various topsoils will be locally where different species are growing.

Fig. 2-1. *Areas are often named for the largest dominant plant species.*

Materials

- two different areas where different
  dominant species are growing
- shovel
- ruler
- pad and pencil

Procedure

Locate two different areas where dominant species are growing, such as a cedar forest and a field of grass for instance. At each site, clear the ground litter (leaves, twigs, bark) off of the surface of the soil. Using a shovel, dig a hole large enough to allow you to measure a cross section of the soil (Fig. 2-2). Draw a picture showing the layers. Photograph it or take a vertical slice of the soil for display in a science fair or classroom presentation. Reach a conclusion about your hypothesis.

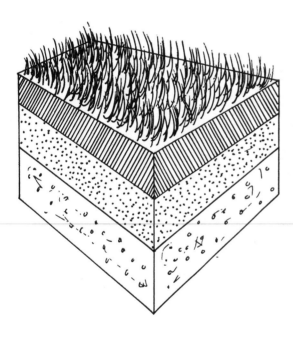

Fig. 2-2. *Examine the vertical cross section of the soil beneath the surface.*

Going Further

1. Get permission to examine the topsoil layer in an orchard and compare it to other areas.

2. Some trees have tap roots that go deep and some have horizontally spreading roots. Do trees that have tap roots require different thickness of topsoil than trees whose roots spread out closer to the surface or is it a function of the level of the water table?

PROJECT 2-3
Feed Me, I'm Hungry

Overview

All soils have nutrients. Some have more than others. All plants have nutritional needs, some more than others. A soil's contents make up one of the factors that determine the species of plants that can live there (climate is an important factor too). You can measure the quantity of nutrients in soil by using test kits. Nitrogen is the single biggest nutrient requirement for most plants. Most soils contain nitrogen. Farmers who try to harvest the same crop year after year in the same soil soon find that the soil is depleted of nitrogen and must be fertilized.

In nature, some soils are nitrogen poor. The plants that live there meet their nitrogen needs by trapping and digesting insects, such as the Venus's-flytrap, the sundew, and the pitcher plant. These insectivorous plants (insect eating) live in swamps and bogs where pH is low. Hypothesize that nitrogen will be lower in soils where insectivorous plants live compared to other soils in forests, plains, or even in your backyard.

Materials

- nitrogen soil test kit
  (see the Resource List for supplier)
- bog area where a carnivorous
  or insectivorous plant is growing
- backyard or other area away from a bog
- shovel and bucket
- paper and pen

Procedure

Using a soil test kit, test and record the nitrogen in several different types of soil, one of which should include a bog area. Compare the results. Verify your results by running the tests twice. If there is a big difference in your results from the first tests, you might need to run further tests. Was your hypothesis correct?

Going Further

1. Using a pH soil test kit, compare the acidity/alkalinity of bog soil to other soils. Would you hypothesize that the differences would be great?

2. Build a bog terrarium and maintain insectivorous plants (available from your local nursery or some of the suppliers listed in the Resource List). Are some plants harder to maintain artificially than others?

PROJECT 2-4
It's Leaking In

Overview

Some plants that grow in lakes and ponds are not rooted, but float freely about. Some plants are rooted but don't reach the water's surface. Others are rooted and grow up to the surface. Underneath a lake there is land. On top of that is litter, but below is soil. Plants root themselves in the soil and grow up through the water, such as lilies (Fig. 2-3). Plants grow up through the water and extend above the surface of the water. How easily does water travel through this type of soil? Hypothesize that water travels faster through soil at the bottom of the lake where vegetation is growing compared to other areas of the lake bottom where no vegetation is growing. You might hypothesize that the opposite is true.

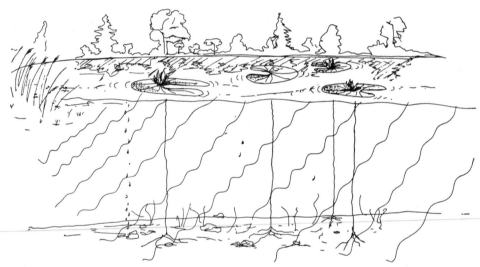

Fig. 2-3. *Lilies are rooted in the soil at the bottom of lakes and ponds.*

Materials

- lake, pond, or stream
- 3″ diameter piece of PVC pipe, about 3 feet long
- hammer
- hand pump or siphon (such as one used by boaters)
- ruler
- marker
- flashlight
- watch
- block of wood (six-inch long piece of 2 × 4)

Procedure

Locate a lake, pond, or stream. Pick a spot where vegetation, such as water lilies, is growing in the lake. In a shallow area where the water is only about two feet deep, rest a three-inch diameter piece of PVC pipe on the lake bottom. Mark the waterline on the pipe. Using a ruler, make a mark on the pipe three inches above the waterline. Drive the pipe three inches down into the ground using a hammer (Fig. 2-4). Place a block of wood over the top of the pipe and strike the wood with the hammer. The wood prevents the pipe from splitting when struck. Next, use a hand siphon to drain the water out of the PVC pipe. Note the time. Water will begin to slowly leak in, filling the pipe (percolation). Because no water can leak in through the pipe itself, the leak is coming from water traveling up through the soil at the bottom of the lake, stream, or pond. Record the length of time it takes to refill the tube.

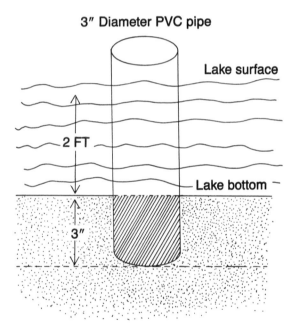

3″ Diameter PVC pipe

Fig. 2-4. *Drive a piece of PVC pipe three inches below the bottom of a lake, stream, or other body of water to test percolation.*

In another area of the lake where no vegetation is growing, repeat the procedure. Compare the difference (if any) in the amount of time required to refill the tube. Was your hypothesis correct?

Going Further

1. Repeat the experiment, comparing lake bottom soil to stream bottom soil or to bog soil.

2. If the water table is close to the surface, dig a hole and perform the experiment only on land. Use a balsa wood float with a long stick attached. As the water level rises, the float will rise and the stick will indicate the amount of rise.

PROJECT 2-5
Rotten to the Core
Adult Supervision Required

Overview

Decaying organic material provides fertilization for plants. It provides a rich source of nutrients. Plants take root and grow in the soil. Hypothesize whether forest soil or soil from an overgrown field contains a greater percentage of organic material. Compare the depth of the humus.

Materials

- shovel
- ruler
- 2 containers (such as large peanut butter jars)
- 2 cookie sheets
- oven
- scale
- labels and pen

Procedure

Locate an area where there is an overgrown field, then locate a heavily wooded area such as a park or forest. At each site, remove the top litter from an area on the ground (leaves, twigs, bark, trash) to expose the topsoil underneath. Using a shovel, remove a small amount of soil (about a three-inch cube). Place it in a container. Do this at both locations. As you dig a hole to remove each sample, measure the depth of the humus (from the surface to a layer of sand).

Spread each sample (the forest sample and the field sample) onto cookie sheets. Be sure to label which sheet holds which sample. Let the moisture dry out of them for a few days. Placing the samples in sunlight might reduce the drying time. When the samples are dry, weigh them on a scale. Record their weight on a chart such as the one shown in Fig. 2-5.

Soil type	Weight before burning	Weight after burning	Percent organic material	Percent inorganic material
Forest				
Field				

Fig. 2-5. *Calculate the percentage of organic material in each sample.*

Remove any large pieces of organic materials such as leaves, twigs, or bark from the soil. Have an adult place the cookie sheets in an oven and broil on a high setting in a vented oven for 7 to 10 minutes. You **must** have an adult help you do this. The material might smoke, creating a potential fire hazard.

Organic matter will be burned away, leaving only inorganic material. After each sample has been heated, let cool and reweigh them. Record the results in the chart. Calculate the percentage of inorganic material in each sample by dividing the weight after heating by the weight before heating. Calculate the percentage of organic material by subtracting the percentage of organic material from 100 (for 100 percent). Record these figures on the chart and conclude whether or not your hypothesis was correct.

Going Further

Using a piece of PVC pipe, take a core sample of a lake bottom at a two-feet deep location. Take samples at other areas around the lake and compare the soil. Which area will have the greatest amount of organic material? Are weather, sunlight, or geographical features important factors?

PROJECT 2-6
Winter Homes
Adult Supervision Required

Overview

Many animals change their metabolism in the winter. They become less active. Some organisms bury themselves under the soil that is at the bottom of lakes and ponds. Hypothesize what the temperature of the soil underneath a lake will be when the surface of the lake is frozen.

Materials

- lake or pond
- cold time in winter when ice has formed on the top of a lake or pond
- thermometer
- broom handle
- duct tape
- ruler
- marker

Procedure

In this project, a thermometer must be lowered several inches into the soil at the bottom of a lake. To do this, wrap duct tape around the bottom and top of the thermometer to the broom handle (keeping the scale uncovered for reading) as shown in Fig. 2-6. Tape it to the bottom section of the broom handle. Using a ruler, mark off one-inch increments on the broom handle.

Fig. 2-6. *Attach the thermometer to the broom handle with tape.*

On a cold winter day when ice has begun to form on the top of a body of fresh water, take your broom handle thermometer to a shallow portion of the water (one- or two-feet deep). Break the ice. Place the broom handle in the water until it rests on the bottom. Note the depth of the water on the broom handle. Watching the inch markings, push the handle down until the thermometer is several inches into the lake bottom. Leave it there for 10 minutes. When you bring the thermometer up, read the temperature on it as quickly as you can, because the temperature will soon change to match the air temperature. Record the soil temperature. Let the thermometer remain in the air for 10 minutes. Record the air temperature. Compare the two temperatures and reach a conclusion concerning your hypothesis. Then go inside for a cup of hot chocolate!

Going Further

1. Record temperatures at different depths in the water and in the soil. Is it warmer as you go down further? Is it colder?
2. Try temperature differences between air and inside hollow logs. What type of organisms might be living there? How about a cave or cedar swamp?

PROJECT 2-7
Pile Driver
Adult Supervision Required

Overview

The grabbing ability of sand around a piling, such as what houses are sometimes built on, is very strong. Is there a relationship between the amount of surface contact made with sand by a piling? Hypothesize that the resistance to movement of a piling due to the force of sand grabbing it in increasing quantities is not "linear." That is to say that if the amount of sand is doubled, and the resistance measured, doubling the sand quantity will more than double the resistance force. The resistance of sand is great. Pile drivers need to use water jets to help push the sand out of the way when they sink pilings in the ground for new home construction at the seashore.

Materials

- spring scale
- three-liter, plastic soda bottle
- piece of wire
- wooden dowel, about 1/4″ in diameter
- sand
- ruler
- drill and scissors
- marker
- pad and pencil

Procedure

Have an adult drill a small hole near one end of a wooden dowel. Tie one end of a piece of wire in it and the other end to a spring scale (Fig. 2-7). Cut the top off of the three-liter, plastic soda bottle with the scissors. Mark one-inch increments on the side of the bottle. Place the wooden dowel upright in the bottom of the bottle. Pour sand into the bottle until it reaches a one-inch depth. Slowly pull the spring scale. Observe and record the amount of force needed to pull the dowel out of the sand. Empty the sand out of the bottle. Stand the dowel upright on the bottom again, and pour two inches of sand into the bottle. Again, record the amount of force needed to move the dowel.

Continue repeating this procedure at one-inch intervals until the bottle is filled with sand. Examine your results and conclude whether or not your hypothesis was correct.

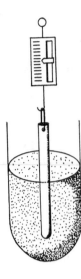

Fig. 2-7. *Construct a device like this one for testing the grabbing ability of sand.*

Going Further

1. Differing diameters of wooden dowels change the amount of surface area that comes in contact with the soil. Is it a function of surface area or shape? Try a flat piece of wood, such as a ruler.

2. Spring scales are sometimes hard to read when you pull on the dowel and suddenly it pops out of the sand. Devise a way to record the maximum force achieved. Place a strip of masking tape on the scale and attach the point of a felt tip pen to the scale's pointer. This will record the maximum force.

3. Will sand particle size make a significant difference?

3

Ecology

Ecology is the relationship of organisms to other organisms and their non-living environment. Ecology deals with the habitat, food chains, birth, death, decaying of once-living organisms, and life cycles. It studies populations of organisms living together in groups or communities. Within communities, some organisms are food producers, while some protect their habitat from predators. Their shelter must be protected from the weather and temperature extremes.

PROJECT 3-1
Cover Up
Adult Supervision Required

Overview

Living organisms need a certain amount of space to live. Can you image living in an elevator with several other people? We can put up with being in tight proximity with other people, but only for a short time. After that, our mental and physical health are affected. Plants need a certain amount of space for their roots to spread out to gather water and nutrients. Reduced habitat creates less population. The dwindling bamboo forests are reducing the number of Panda "bears."

Hypothesize that there is a relationship between habitat size and the number of organisms living there.

Materials

- 1 × 1 square foot piece of plywood
- 2 × 2 square foot piece of plywood
- 4 × 4 square foot piece of plywood
- section of backyard lawn or forest area
- small gardner's hand shovel
- handsaw

Procedure

Measure and mark three pieces of plywood, 1 × 1, 2 × 2, and 4 × 4 square foot pieces, then have an adult cut them for you. On an undisturbed section of lawn in your backyard, lay each board flatly on the ground. Leave at least a three foot space between each board. After one or two weeks, remove the one foot square board. Count the number of organisms you find living under it. Record them in the chart shown in Fig. 3-1.

Organism	1 × 1 Quantity	2 × 2 Quantity	4 × 4 Quantity
worms			
larvae			
grubs			
centipedes			
others			

Fig. 3-1. *A home for a number of organisms.*

Similarly, remove the 2 × 2 board and the 4 × 4 board and observe the number of living organisms. Examine your results and conclude whether or not population is directly related to habitat.

Going Further

A friend of ours was given a six-inch long pet alligator 30 years ago. It grew until it was as big as it could comfortably fit in the tank, then it seemed to stop growing. When they placed it in a larger tank, it began to grow again but stopped when it reached a size where it was becoming cramped. Other pet-shop fish, such as Oscars and Black Sharks, will grow bigger if they are housed in a bigger aquarium. Hypothesize that reduced habitat can also result in reduced size of some animals.

PROJECT 3-2

Longer in the Womb, Later to the Tomb

Overview

"Gestation period" is the time it takes a female animal to carry its baby until it is ready to be born. Different animals require different lengths of time to produce offspring. Mammals carry their babies in wombs. Turtles and chickens lay eggs, which take a certain length of time to hatch. Human beings take nine months from the time of conception until a baby is born. Elephants have a gestation period of 20 to 22 months.

If an animal has a long gestation period, will it have a long life span? Hypothesize that species of animals whose gestation period is relatively long, live longer lives compared to species whose gestation period is shorter.

Materials

- Research books containing information on the gestation periods and longevity of many animals, birds, and insects.

Procedure

This project requires researching information in books, compiling the data, and examining that data on a chart in which you record the data (Fig. 3-2). Research the gestation period and longevity of a wide variety of animal life: elephants, turtles, chickens, insects, birds, etc. Try to study a wide range of animals and animal types: reptiles, mammals, and amphibians. Gather the data and use the chart for recording. Study the data, and reach a conclusion about your hypothesis.

Organism	Gestation period	Longevity
elephant	20 – 22 months	60 years

Fig. 3-2. *Gestation period and longevity of animals.*

Going Further

1. The number of offspring is related to the number of things that feed on it (predators). Hypothesize that when the quantity of offspring is high the survival rate of eggs or newborn offspring is poor. Salmon, for example, lay 50,000 eggs, but there are a lot of things that eat the eggs and young salmon. In the plant kingdom, orchids produce four or five million seeds but their requirements for growth are so demanding that very few seeds produce new plants.

PROJECT 3-3
"Wood" It Burn Well
Adult Supervision Required

Overview

When trees die, they naturally decompose and return nutrients to the ground. Trees can sometimes be dead and yet still be standing. Are there any factors that make trees decompose quicker when they are lying on the ground than when they are standing dead? Hypothesize that wood lying on the ground decomposes faster than dead standing wood. If this is true, then it is important that owners of fireplaces and wood stoves know this. Dead wood should be picked up as soon as it falls if it is to be used for burning to provide heat, because as wood decomposes, its ability to give off heat is reduced.

Materials

- dead standing tree
- dead tree lying on the ground
  (which is the same species as the dead standing tree)
- saw
- bathroom scale

Procedure

Locate a dead tree that is still standing. Locate a tree that is dead but lying on the ground. It must be the same species as the one standing. Carefully cut about a two-foot long section off of each tree. Be sure to get permission if the trees are not on your own property.

You want to determine which wood is denser, the one that is standing or the one that's been on the ground for a while. This can be done by measuring the radius of the log (one half the diameter), squaring that number, multiplying the result by 3.14 (pi) and by the length. The formula is:

$$3.14 \times \text{radius}^2 \times \text{length} = \text{volume}$$

If the log has a radius of two inches and is 20 inches long, then:

$$3.14 \times 2^2 \text{ inches} \times 20 \text{ inches} = \text{volume}$$
$$251.2 \text{ cubic inches} = \text{volume}$$

Now that you know the area, or volume, you can come up with a number to represent density by dividing the volume by the weight. In the case of our example:

$$251.2 \div \text{weight}$$

Do these measurements and computations on both logs. Which is more dense? Was your hypothesis correct? As a tree deteriorates, it will give off less heat when it is used as firewood.

Going Further

1. Measure nitrogen in the soil both at a spot in the forest where there are trees, but no dead, fallen wood, and in an area where rotting logs are found. Use a nitrogen test kit (see the Source List for a list of science equipment suppliers).

2. Identify the rate of decomposition of both standing dead wood and wood lying on the ground. Perform the above experiment. Use a ribbon to mark the standing tree and the tree on the ground to later identify them. Go back to the trees several months later. Again, cut pieces of each (cut the first few inches off first to remove any weather-affected pieces) and perform the experiment's computations. Compare the results and see which tree is decomposing faster.

PROJECT 3-4
Hair Helps
Adult Supervision Required

STOP

Overview

Heat and cold are a big part of our environment. Organisms have different ways of dealing with excessive temperatures. The greatest heat loss for humans is from the top of their heads. Hypothesize that hair acts as an insulator and helps maintain our body temperature.

Materials

- human hair
- heat lamp
- two thermometers
- two cloth bags (or handkerchiefs with safety pins to form a bag)
- clock

Procedure

Set up the heat lamp as shown in Fig. 3-3. Gather some hair (a barber shop or beauty salon should have plenty). Using safety pins and either two

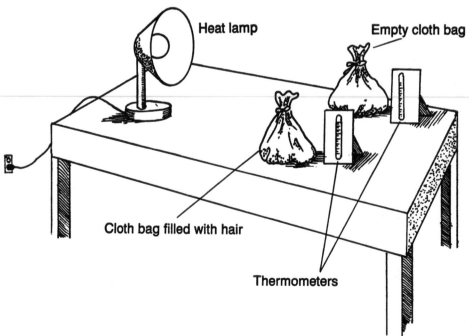

Fig. 3-3. *The setup for determining the insulating effect of hair.*

Time	Thermometer uninsulated	Thermometer insulated
zero	(room temp)	(room temp)
After 10 minutes		
After 20 minutes		
After 30 minutes		

Fig. 3-4. *Recording temperature data.*

handkerchiefs or two squares of cloth, make two "sandwich bag" size bags. Fill one with hair. Leave the other one empty. Place the thermometers on a table three feet from the heat lamp. In front of one thermometer, place the bag of hair. In front of the other thermometer, place the empty cloth bag. This bag will be the control. Both thermometers should read the same room temperature. Turn on the heat lamp. **Be very careful. Heat lamps become very hot**. Observe each thermometer. Use the chart shown in Fig. 3-4 to record the temperatures as time passes. Examine your data and conclude whether or not your hypothesis was correct.

Going Further

Put other insulators in the bags for testing. The Indians use adobe clay as an insulator. Use pink, spun glass insulation found in homes. Feathers insulate ducks, chickens, and other birds.

PROJECT 3-5
Blubber Is Beautiful

Overview

Many animals have a thick layer of lard (fat) to protect them from the cold. In the sea, air-breathing mammals, such as seals, walruses, whales, and dolphins, maintain their warm body temperatures by their insulating fat.

This project demonstrates that fat keeps cold out. Hypothesize that lard will insulate against cold.

Materials

- 2 coffee mugs
- 2 pieces of cardboard, about 3″ square
- 2 thermometers
- cup of shortening or lard
- clock
- refrigerator or cold area

Procedure

Fill a coffee mug with shortening, the sticky, white substance used in cooking. Cut a small hole in each of the two three-inch square pieces of cardboard. Place a thermometer in each hole. The holes should be small enough to snugly hold the thermometers. Position the thermometers through each piece of cardboard so that their bulbs are suspended in the middle of the cups when the cardboard sheets are placed over the top (Fig. 3-5). You do not want the thermometers to touch the bottom or sides of the cups.

Let the cups sit until they are both at room temperature, then place them both in a refrigerator. If it is cold outside, do the experiment outdoors. Using the chart in Fig. 3-6, observe and record the temperature on the two thermometers as different time intervals.

Study the data you collected, and conclude whether your hypothesis was correct.

Going Further

Perform the experiment starting with cold temperatures and increasing to warm temperatures. Compare the amount of time for both cups to go from room temperature to identical cold temperatures, to the amount of time beginning at a cold temperature and rising to room temperature. Would you expect one time to be longer than another?

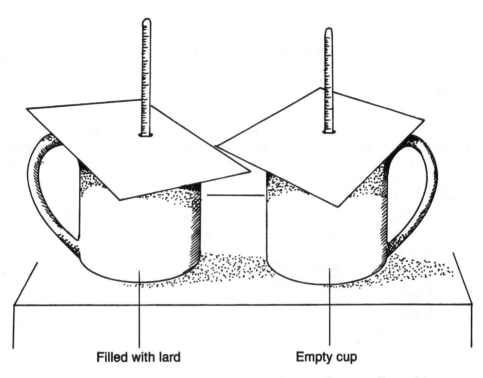

Fig. 3-5. *The setup for determining the insulating effect of fat.*

Time	Thermometer uninsulated	Thermometer insulated
zero	(room temp)	(room temp)
After 10 minutes		
After 20 minutes		
After 30 minutes		

Fig. 3-6. *Recording temperature data.*

PROJECT 3-6
Chicken Feed Is for the Birds

Overview

Animal populations are directly related to their food supply. The Koala "bear" population would vanish if eucalyptus trees disappeared. Hypothesize that a particular bird that lives in your area will be attracted to a particular type of food.

Materials

- 6 aluminum pie plates with holes in them
- 3, two-liter plastic soda bottles with metal caps
- scissors
- 3 bolts and 6 corresponding nuts
- mixed bag of wild bird seed
  (from a pet shop or supermarket)
- string
- tree with limbs to
  hang three bird feeders
- brass paper fasteners
- bird identification book
- binoculars (optional)
- box of crackers

Procedure

Construct three identical bird feeders like the ones shown in Fig. 3-7a and 3-7b. Exercise care when using sharp scissors. Instructions for building them follows.

Cut the bottom off of a two-liter plastic soda bottle. Discard the bottom part. Cut one-inch long tabs in four equally spaced "sides" of the bottle to secure to the pie plate. These tabs will be pushed through slots cut in an aluminum pie plate and fastened to it. The bird food will rest in the pie plate and the holes in the plate will let rain drain through. In the spaces between each tab, cut small "V" shaped openings. You will fill the bottle with bird seed and the seed will come out the openings as the birds eat it. Carefully cut four slots in a pie plate that line up with the four tabs in the bottle. Push the tabs through the slots in the pie plate. Fold each tab up under the pie plate. Cautiously punch a small hole with the end of the pair of scissors (or an awl) in each tab and through the pie plate. Place a brass paper fastener through each to hold them together. This makes the bird feeder base.

Carefully punch a hole in a soda bottle cap, then punch a hole in the center of a pie plate. This pie plate will go on top of the feeder and help shelter the food from rain. Place a bolt up through the inside of the cap and

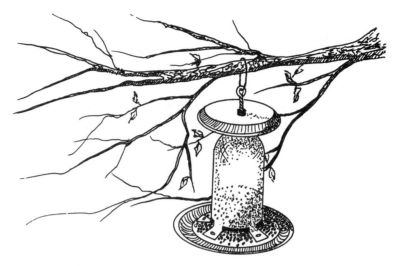

Fig. 3-7A. *A constructed bird feeder.*

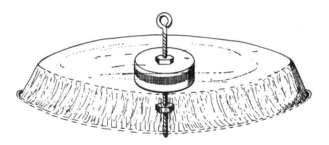

Fig. 3-7B. *Close-up of the lid construction.*

through the pie plate resting on top (see Fig. 3-7b). Screw a nut onto the bolt to hold the pie plate to the bottle cap. Tie a piece of string around the bolt. Screw another nut on top of the existing nut to secure the string tied between them. The other end of the string will eventually be tied to a tree limb.

Construct two more identical bird feeders.

Separate the mixed bird seeds into piles, putting each kind in its own pile. You will need two types of seed. If you can purchase two bags of individual seeds (not mixed) instead of buying a mixed bag, do so.

Fill one feeder with one type of seed. Fill the second with another type. Fill the third with crushed crackers. Tie the three feeders to a tree limb. If possible, place them in view from a window in the house where you can make daily observations perhaps near a window where you can watch while you eat meals.

What types of birds come to feed at which feeders? Identify the species. Do some species of birds eat at more than one feeder or do they always eat from the same one? After much observation and note taking, conclude whether your hypothesis was correct.

Going Further

1. Experiment with other types of seeds and bird food.

2. Can you adapt an animal to a different diet? Offer a pet mouse a little of his normal food and a lot of something similar but not his favorite. Will he begin to eat his second choice? Do not endanger its life.

PROJECT 3-7
Who Comes to Drink

Overview

Some insects and animals are attracted to sweetness. Bees, for example, like the sweet nectar of flowers. In this project, a pan containing a mixture of sugar water will be set outdoors in an observable area. Knowing the types of animals and insects that live in your area, hypothesize which organisms will come to drink the sugar water in the daytime and which will come in the darkness of night (some animals are nocturnal).

Materials

- sugar and water
- spoon
- aluminum pie plate
- small gardening shovel
- small area of ground (in the backyard)

Procedure

Using a small, hand-gardening shovel, dig a hole in the ground and place a pie plate in it so that the top lip of the plate is at ground level. This will ensure that crawling creatures can easily drink from the plate. Mix several teaspoons of sugar into the pie pan filled with water. At various times of the day and evening, examine the "oasis" and see if anything is drinking. Identify the organism and conclude whether your hypothesis was correct.

Going Further

1. Build a perimeter of mud about two-feet thick around the outside of the pan so footprints are left if larger animals like rodents or mammals come while you are gone.

2. Set out another pie plate containing only water in addition to the sugar water plate to see if a species is attracted because of the sweetness or simply because of the water.

4

Pests and Controls

The name "pest" is often given to someone or something that is a nuisance or causes trouble. In the animal kingdom, a pest is an organism that annoys your garden, such as caterpillars eating leaves in a vegetable garden. Rabbits can be pests in a garden too. Sea gulls are large beautiful birds, but they sometimes harass people for food. Pests can be diseases that attack plants. In the plant kingdom, pests can be "weeds." Weeds are unwanted plants. Any plant growing outside of the desired plant species is a weed. A rose growing in a barley field is a weed, even though roses are prized flowers. When a pine plantation is maintained, oak trees are considered to be weeds and are removed.

The terms "weed" and "pest" are not always easily defined. In a lawn, some people consider dandelions to be weeds while other people enjoy their yellow flower. A lot of people think of bats and spiders as being pests, but they actually provide a service to humans by eating undesirable insects. So whether something is a pest or a weed depends on the particular circumstances and how an individual feels about the organism.

Nature has ways of dealing with pests. Basil grown parallel to tomato plants repels flies, mosquitos, and certain diseases. Bay (or laurel) leaves eliminates weevils when stored along with grains such as corn, oat, and rye. Bush beans and potatoes planted in alternate rows help each other survive. The beans keep Colorado potato beetles out of the potatoes and the potatoes keep Mexican bean beetles out of the beans. This is called "companion planting."

PROJECT 4-1
Insect Picnic

Overview

No matter where you are, outdoor picnics usually bring uninvited pests. Can you set out a bait to attract insect pests? If so, it could be placed a little away from your picnic table to keep pests from bothering you. In this project you will make several solutions to attempt to make bait for insects. Hypothesize which one (if any) will best lure picnic insect pests and reduce the number around the picnic table.

Materials

- water
- four pie plates
- cola
- honey
- spoon
- insect identification book

Procedure

Fill a pie plate with water. Fill a second pie plate with cola. Fill two more pie plates with water. Add several teaspoons of sugar to one of the water-filled plates and mix until it is all dissolved. Mix several teaspoons of honey into another water-filled plate. Set all four pie plates outdoors in an area where there are a lot of insect pests (Fig. 4-1). Observe and record your data. To present your results to others, you might want to label the

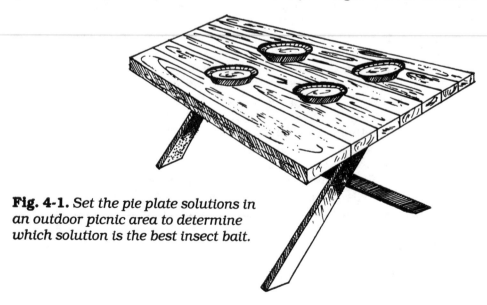

Fig. 4-1. Set the pie plate solutions in an outdoor picnic area to determine which solution is the best insect bait.

pans then photograph your experiment. Conclude whether your hypothesis was correct.

Going Further

1. Dig four slight depressions in the ground and place the pie plates solutions in them so the lip of the plates is at ground level. What type of "creepy-crawly" insects are attracted to the solutions?

2. Locate an ant hill. Mark off a square yard area around the ant hill with the hill in the middle. At each corner of the square, place one of the pie plates. Which mixture attracts the ants and which repels them? Let the plates remain in the ground for a day or two until the ants discover their presence. Observe their behavior.

3. If your bait doesn't keep the insects away, identify what picnic items they are attracted to. What bait is good?

PROJECT 4-2
Nighttime Flyers
Adult Supervision Required

Overview

Many animals, such as moths, are nocturnal, that is, they sleep in the day and become active at night. They can often be seen fluttering around outdoor lights. Propane lanterns used by campers produce both heat and light. Are the insects attracted to the heat of the bulbs or to the light? Hypothesize whether heat or light are the biggest attraction for flying insects.

Materials

- flashlight
- iron (used to iron clothing)
- heavy-duty extension cord

Procedure

This project is best done on an evening when the moon is bright. It should be a still, windless summer night. Set a flashlight (which gives off light but almost no heat) in an area where flying insects are common. Three feet away, stand up an iron (Fig. 4-2). Turn it on to radiate heat (Warning: fire and burn hazard). Observe which nocturnal insects are attracted to the light or the iron and record your data. Was your hypothesis correct?

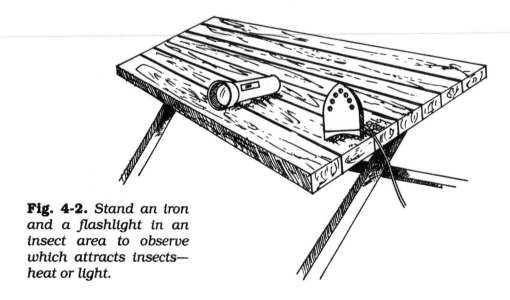

Fig. 4-2. *Stand an iron and a flashlight in an insect area to observe which attracts insects—heat or light.*

Going Further

1. Aim a flashlight at a white piece of cloth, such as a tee-shirt. Are insects attracted to the light, to the cloth, or both?

2. Put a piece of black paper on a white ceiling over the top of a lamp where gnats frequently gather at night. Does color have any effect on attracting gnats? Use different colors.

PROJECT 4-3
Window Box Protection

Overview

Marigolds have a very strong scent. It has long been known that planting marigolds around a garden helps control some pests. Some insects such as gnats are so tiny that screens do not keep them out. Will marigolds help repel gnats? If so, a window box planter might keep gnats away from open windows. Form a hypothesis and test it.

Materials

- various pieces of lumber
  (to construct a simple window box)
- marigolds
- potting soil
- 2 lamps

Procedure

Using several pieces of wood, construct a simple window box. Mount it on a window in a room that has several windows. Plant marigolds in it (Fig. 4-3).

Fig. 4-3. *Can the scent of marigolds in a window box repel gnats?*

Place a lamp near the window where a window box is mounted. On the same side of the building, place another lamp next to another window. On the evening when the gnat population is high (around the middle of June where we live), open the windows in the room and turn on the lights. After a period of time, observe the quantity of gnats on the ceiling and conclude whether your hypothesis was correct.

Going Further

1. What flying insects, if any, do marigolds repel?

2. Experiment with different scented plants and other materials.

PROJECT 4-4
Scare Bottles
Adult Supervision Required

Overview

Everyone is familiar with scarecrows, which farmers place in their fields to keep birds away. Is it the motion of the scarecrow blowing in the wind that scares the birds? The home gardener has the same problem with birds. Hypothesize that it is the motion of the object that keeps birds away. In this project, you will construct a motion device from an empty plastic soda bottle and test its effectiveness.

Cities don't want pigeons. They are pests. If you prove your device to be workable, then this would offer a recycling use for plastic soda bottles.

Materials

- 2, two-liter, plastic soda bottles
- long wooden dowel (about three feet)
- garden, lawn, birdbath, or area
  near your home where birds regularly gather
- scissors or utility knife
- glue

Procedure

Locate an area around your home where birds regularly gather. This area should be easily seen from a window in your home to allow easy observation. The area could be a small garden plot, a lawn, or a birdbath. You can use food as bait to attract the birds.

This project requires three weeks of observations and recordings. First, observe the area for a 15 minute period in the morning and a 15 minute period later in the day. Most birds begin to feed within an hour or two after dawn. This might be your best observation time in the morning. Determine the average number of birds that visit per 15 minute period.

During the project, also make note of the weather. Will the varying weather conditions affect your results? Study your results. Was your hypothesis correct?

Using a pair of scissors or a utility knife, carefully cut four 2″ × 6″ strips out of the side of a plastic soda bottle. Glue these strips on opposite sides on another two-liter plastic soda bottle (Fig. 4-4). These flaps will catch the wind. Cut a hole in the bottom of the soda bottle. Keep the screw cap on top of the bottle. Place a wooden dowel in the ground in the area where the birds gather. Stick the bottle on top of the dowel (Fig. 4-4).

At the end of the first week of observation, place your homemade scare-bottle device in the ground plot. Tie it up so that it will not spin or

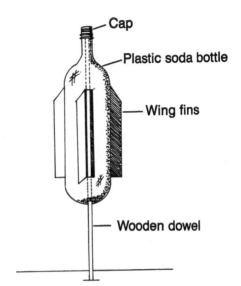

Fig. 4-4. *Testing the effectiveness of a modern scarecrow made by recycling plastic soda bottles.*

Labels: Cap, Plastic soda bottle, Wing fins, Wooden dowel

make any movement. Again watch the plot for a week, 15 minutes in the morning and 15 minutes late in the day. At the same time each day, observe as you did the first week. Record your observations. This week's observations will show if the birds have any response to the presence of the scare bottle.

For the third and final week, untie the scare bottle and let it rotate freely. Observe daily and record your results.

Going Further

1. Is the speed of rotation a factor in scaring birds away?

2. Do birds learn that there is no hazard in the wind-bottle device? Can you add streamers to it to make it more scary to them?

3. Determine the range of effectiveness of the bottle device. Are some species of birds more wary than others? Can you increase the range of its effectiveness? How? Paint eyes on it to look like an owl.

4. Can small holes be made in the solid walls of the scare bottle to make a sound that scares birds? It need not produce a sound within the range of human hearing.

PROJECT 4-5
Crabby Grass

Overview

An attractive and healthy lawn is usually free of "weeds." Typically, weeds in the form of dandelions, crabgrass, chickweed, and clover try to crowd out the blades of grass. Can any of these weeds be reduced simply by watering the lawn more or perhaps less? If a lawn could be watered a little more than normal to prevent some weeds, and still maintain the healthy grass, then this would be an inexpensive and natural weed control. Form a hypothesis.

Materials

- garden hose and water supply
- weed identification book
- dozen small wooden stakes
- string or thin rope
- lawn
- tarp or waterproof cover
  (one square yard or larger)

Procedure

Stake out three plots on a lawn. Each plot should be one square yard in size and should be separated from the other plots by several feet. Identify and count the number of weeds in each plot and record them in the chart shown in Fig. 4-5.

	Dandelions	Crab grass	Chick weed	Clover
Before				
After				

Fig. 4-5. *Chart for recording data for the project* Crabby Grass.

One plot will receive watering naturally from the weather. Another plot will receive heavy daily watering from you, and the third will only receive enough water to prevent the grass from suffering. You will have to place a plastic sheet or tarp over this plot when it rains and remove it when the rain stops.

After several weeks, count the number of weeds again in each plot and record your data in the chart. Conclude whether your hypothesis was correct.

Going Further

1. Try other natural substances as weed killers. Pour a cup of tea steeped with two tea bags onto the square foot plot each day.

2. Evaluate a lawn and attempt to determine why some areas are weed free.

PROJECT 4-6
Netting Your Food

Overview

Many people do not like spiders and consider them pests. However, spiders provide a service to humans. They eat many of the insects that bother people. Hypothesize that the size of a spider is directly related to the number of insects it catches. The larger the spider, the more it needs to eat, so perhaps it needs a larger web (or one that is more efficient or in a better location).

Materials

- several spider webs
- drawing pens and paper
- an insect identification book

Procedure

Locate several spider webs. Draw a spider web map as shown in Fig. 4-6, one for each web. Over a period of two weeks, observe each web daily and record the location of any insects caught within the web and the date of the catch. Identify the type of insect caught in the web. You might want to make two observations each day, one in the morning and one in the evening. Study your data and conclude whether your hypothesis was correct.

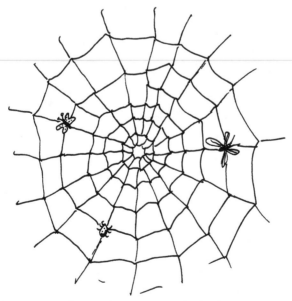

Fig. 4-6. *Using a spider web map, track daily catches in the web.*

Going Further

1. At the end of the observation period, break the spider web. See if it is reconstructed overnight. If not, how long before it is reconstructed?

2. Using an identification book of spiders, identify each species of spider by the spider and by the type of web it weaves.

3. Is it true that the larger the spider the larger the web?

PROJECT 4-7
Nature's Herbicide
Adult Supervision Required

Overview

Some plants release chemicals that prevent other plants from growing nearby, such as the Black Walnut tree. Black Walnut trees produce a tannin that prevents other plants, including other Black Walnuts, from growing nearby. The leaves might decompose to produce an acid, or the roots might release an acid. In this experiment, you will try to obtain some of this acid. Hypothesize that the acid can be poured on weeds to prevent their growth.

Materials

- 30 to 50 leaves from a Black Walnut tree
- 10-quart pot
- draining spoon
- stove
- gallon milk or juice jug (plastic or glass)
- weeds growing around your house

Procedure

After the leaves have been gathered, fill the pot half full with leaves then fill the pot with water to about two inches from the top. Have an adult boil the water and leaf mixture for about 10 minutes. Be very careful handling the hot pot and the very hot water.

	Weed with solution	Weed with water	Weed with nothing added
Day 1			
Day 2			
Day 3			
Day 4			
Day 5			
Day 6			
Day 7			

Fig. 4-7. *Chart for recording data in the project* Nature's Herbicide.

Remove the leaves with the draining spoon. Put the remaining half of the leaves into the hot water. Bring the water to the boiling point again and boil for 10 more minutes.

Remove this batch of leaves. Boil the solution until there is only about one quart of liquid remaining. Allow the solution to cool. When it is at room temperature, pour the solution into a clean bottle.

Locate weeds around your property. Each day at dusk, pour about 2 ounces of the solution on the weed. Pour only on those days when it has not rained. On another weed, pour only water. You can also choose a third weed as a control plant. Do not water it or give it any attention at all.

Make observations and record you data in the chart shown in Fig. 4-7. After all of the solution has been used, determine whether your hypothesis was correct. Would this be a practical method for weed control?

Going Further

1. Would more leechate be extracted if nuts, roots, bark, or twigs from the Black Walnut tree were used in the mixture?

2. Does the solution work better on specific plants?

5

Recycling

We live in a closed environment. We only have the resources of this planet at our disposal (at least for the present). If we and future generations are to continue to live here, we must make wise decisions regarding the use of all of Earth's resources. Unfortunately, societies are driven by economics. The intense desire to make money at both the personal and the corporate level often forces conflicts with goals to protect the environment. No ecological choices can be made which do not directly affect an economy.

We live in a "throw away" society. Many items we use are thrown away when we are finished with them—disposable razors, milk jugs, packaging, even small appliances. In fact, some products are designed to become obsolete and not last very long (called "planned obsolescence"). Today, if an inexpensive toaster breaks, many people will simply throw it out and purchase a new one. People used to spend more effort repairing things than they do today.

It is the challenge of our society to begin taking a different view of how we make and use the products we have. Is it possible to reuse some things that we might otherwise discard? Could telephones be made out of something biodegradable, such as wood instead of plastic, which doesn't decompose quickly? In this chapter, we want to stimulate your thinking along the lines of reusing materials and products to help conserve our nation's (and the world's) natural resources. Maybe some of the things that are difficult to decompose should not be made at all.

PROJECT 5-1
Garbage Away!

Overview

Many things we throw away can be returned to the earth to decompose and provide rich nutrients to the soil. The Amish, a religious group in Pennsylvania, are famous for being in touch with the earth. They reuse the manure from their horses to fertilize their farmland. Their society wastes very little.

Much of what we throw away in our garbage can be returned to the earth to provide nutrients for the soil rather than be disposed of in a landfill.

Hypothesize that a significant part (over 30 percent) of the trash that we throw away could be recycled or is biodegradable and could be returned to the earth.

Materials

- kitchen scale (or small postal scale)
- bathroom scale
- small, brown lunch bags
- paper and pen

Procedure

In this project, each item that is thrown in the trash by your family at home will be evaluated and recorded. For a period of one week, have each member of the household place their trash in paper bags for you to weigh, categorize, and record. Use the log in Fig. 5-1 to record the data. Make copies of the log, before you use it because many pages will be needed to record all of the items discarded during the week.

Item name	Weight	Category

Fig. 5-1. *Chart for evaluating household trash in the project* Garbage Away!

Notice on the log that each item disposed of requires the entry of the item name, its weight, and its category. Use a small kitchen scale or postal scale to weigh little amounts of refuse. Each item can be classified in one of several categories. The categories we suggest are:

1. **Able to be recycled.** These are items that we currently have the technology to use over again such as paper, glass, and aluminum.

2. **Able to be used by someone else.** An appliance that could be repaired at a reasonable cost and could continue to give service would fit in this category.

3. **Biodegradable.** Leftover meal scraps, banana peels, dead leaves picked off of house plants, all could be composted or placed in the ground to break down into nutrients, enriching the soil.

4. **Impossible to deal with.** An old telephone that no longer works and is uneconomical to repair, or due to obsolescence, the parts are no longer available, might qualify as a necessary item to take to a dump.

5. **Toxic.** Some dangerous products and substances cannot be re-used and should be disposed of in special ways. Batteries, for example, contain acid and should not be buried in a landfill, because the acid could leech out and contaminate a water supply.

After itemizing a week's refuse, evaluate the data you have collected. What percentage (by weight) of the total disposed material was made up of recyclable and biodegradable items? Was your hypothesis correct or incorrect?

Going Further

1. Environmental awareness in your family can be brought to light by you. Show your family the data you have collected. Does it change their buying and disposing habits. (Note that this project could come under the classification of behavioral science.)

2. Can you incorporate this into a science club project at school where many families are evaluated besides just your own?

PROJECT 5-2
Rip It, Tear It, Discard It

Overview

Land use is at a premium. Recycling paper saves many trees from needing to be cut down. Does recycled paper, that is, paper that has been made from discarded paper products, break down in the soil faster than manufactured paper? If it does, this would be an extra benefit to using recycled paper. Hypothesize that recycled paper biodegrades faster (or slower) than manufactured paper, thus taking up landfill space for a shorter period of time.

Materials

- sheet of manufactured paper
- sheet of recycled paper
- small plot of soil
  (backyard, about 2 foot square)
- small shovel

Procedure

Take a sheet of manufactured paper, say $8^1/2'' \times 11''$, and a sheet of paper made from recycled paper. Dig a hole about two-inches deep and wide enough to lay each piece of paper side by side. Place the sheets next to each other in the hole and cover them over with soil. Draw a diagram indicating the location of the samples.

After one month, carefully remove the sheets. Closely examine the condition of each. Does one look like it has decomposed more than the other? Was your hypothesis correct?

Going Further

1. Does the amount of moisture affect decomposition? In a controlled environment, change the rate of moisture, making more or less, and compare the results.

2. How long does it take for the samples to decompose completely? How do you define decomposition?

PROJECT 5-3
My Old Shirt

Overview

When we think about recycling the products we use, most people tend to think of paper, cardboard, glass, and metal objects, but what about clothing? We all wear clothes. We all buy clothes several times a year. What happens to old clothes? A few articles might be used as dust and cleaning rags around the house. Perhaps some will be passed down to other members of our family and friends. Maybe some will wind up in a Salvation Army box. But where do they go from there? Eventually, they end up in a landfill, even if we don't see it.

Today, much of our clothing is made from man-made materials: rayon, orlon, dacron, and acrylic. How do these substances affect our environment? Do they decompose naturally and return harmless (or even beneficial) nutrients to the soil, or are they like plastic and take up valuable landfill space for hundreds of years? Hypothesize that clothes made from natural substances (cotton, wool, linen, silk) decompose quicker and more efficiently than clothing made from man-made fibers (dacron, polyester).

Materials

- old tee-shirt
- old nylon stockings
- old wool socks or wool yarn
- old acrylic sweater
- soil (a spot in your backyard)
- water
- 4 glass jar containers with lids (mayonnaise jars)
- masking tape and marker

Procedure

Obtain two articles of clothing or material from purely natural substances, such as cotton and wool. Obtain two articles of clothing or material made from man-made fibers, such as nylon and acrylic. Cut three pieces from each material. The pieces should be cut in four-inch squares.

Bury one of each sample material in the ground. You should have a way to identify each piece of material so you will know which is which when you dig them up at a later date. They might be different colors or you could cut them into different shapes for identification, square for nylon, triangle for wool, circle for cotton, rectangle for acrylic. Also place one of each sample material in a glass jar, fill with water, and cover with a lid. Label each jar with masking tape, identifying the type of material that is in it. Place the jars inside your house in a spot out of the sunlight (light encourages algae growth). Place a sample of each indoors on a table or dresser where they can remain undisturbed for a month. These will be the control samples. Again, if the materials are similar in appearance, you might make them distinguishable by cutting them into specific shapes.

After a month, excavate the samples from the soil and remove the samples from the bottle. Compare the deterioration of each sample to the control materials. Was your hypothesis correct? Do you feel society should be allowed to make clothes out of products that we can't get rid of?

Going Further

1. Compare combinations of materials for decomposition. Clothing often contains a combination of natural and man-made fibers (wool and dacron) as well as combinations of man-made fibers (polyester and rayon). Some people are allergic to substances such as rayon. Women's blouses are often made from polyester.

2. Are man-made clothing materials stronger than clothing made from natural substances? Measure the strength needed to pull fibers apart. Develop a process and procedure to measure the strength.

PROJECT 5-4
How Does Your Garden Grow

Overview

The number of chemical combinations man has invented is staggering, and it continues to grow each year. Many of the common, every-day items we use are made from these chemicals: clothing, appliances, food wrappers, and containers. Do these items decompose naturally when buried in a landfill or will they remain as they are for long periods of time? In this project we will plant a "throw away" garden.

Hypothesize that things made purely from substances in nature break down faster than things made from man-made chemical combinations.

Materials

- 2 paper lunch bags
- 2 plastic sandwich bags
- 2 plastic pens
- 2 wooden pencils
- 2 paper plates
- 2 styrofoam plates
- small plot of outside soil (backyard)

Procedure

Many things we use are made of both natural substances and man-made substances. For example, disposable picnic plates can be made of paper or styrofoam. Writing implements (pens and pencils) can be plastic or wood. Bags (sandwich, shopping, etc.) can be either paper or plastic.

Gather two of each item in the materials list. Place one of each kind in a drawer in your room. These will be the control items. Bury one of each item in your backyard. After one month, carefully dig up the buried items. Compare them to the control items. Which items showed signs of decomposition? Was your hypothesis correct?

Going Further

1. Do the project again using other sets of common items we use every day, real houseplants and plastic, artificial plants, wax paper that sticks of butter come wrapped in and plastic tubs of butter.

2. Bury an inner tube, a piece of leather, shoes, and a rubber band.

3. Try to find a product that comes in three types of containers, aluminum, tin alloy, and glass. Use a magnet to tell if a can is aluminum (nonmagnetic) or a tin alloy (magnetic). Many canned products come in tin alloy cans instead of aluminum, as do sodas. Why don't manufacturers use aluminum cans as containers for all vegetables and fruit?

PROJECT 5-5
It's in the Bag

Overview

Nature recycles its own organic materials naturally. Horses feed on grass. The waste from the horse fertilizes and returns nutrients to the soil to stimulate more grass growth. Countless examples can be seen where organisms feed, produce waste, die, and decompose, which is all part of nature's reusing organic material over and over again.

Much decomposition in nature is done by bacteria. These microscopic organisms can be dangerous, causing disease such as scarlet fever, tetanus, and pneumonia. But useful bacteria, which are harmless to humans, help in the decay of dead animal and plant material. This material is decomposed into the soil and gases into the atmosphere. Then these materials are reused as nutrients to produce food for other living organisms.

Hypothesize that bacteria breaks down organic matter, even if oxygen is not present. Bacteria that need air to live are called "aerobic." Bacteria that can survive in the absence of air are "anaerobic."

Materials

- 2 slices of white bread
- 2 clear mayonnaise jars
- 2 plastic resealable sandwich bags
- cheesecloth
- rubber band
- water
- butter knife

Procedure

Take two slices of white bread. Carefully cut a three-inch square from each piece (be careful when using a knife). One side of each sample square should include the crust. Place one bread sample in each plastic, resealable sandwich bag. Add just enough tap water to each bag to make the bread wet (no more than about 1/8 an inch of water in the bottom of the bags).

Squeeze as much air out of one of the bags as you can and seal it tight. After a while, the oxygen that remains will be used by the reaction of decomposing. The other bread sample will be exposed to the air. But we do not want any foreign substances to fall into the bag. To screen out unwanted particles, place the plastic bag in a mayonnaise jar, folding the top of the bag down around the top of the jar. Place a piece of cheesecloth over the top. Use a rubber band to hold the cheesecloth and plastic bag in place (Fig. 5-2). The jar acts as a clear support structure only.

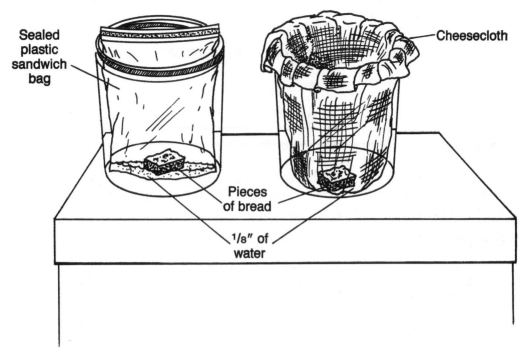

Fig. 5-2. *Comparing the decomposing ability of aerobic and anaerobic bacteria.*

Place both samples in a dark area that is at, or below, room temperature. Make daily observations. Conclude whether your hypothesis was correct.

Going Further

1. Perform the experiment using different organic materials, such as parts of plants and meat.

2. Create an anaerobic decay with biodegradable materials and nonbiodegradable materials (such as shredded plastic bottles). Will the materials that are seemingly nonbiodegradable break down anaerobically? Use an aerobic control.

3. Is temperature a factor? Does it affect aerobic or anaerobic organisms?

PROJECT 5-6
Trees Please (Many Organisms)

Overview

Trees naturally recycle themselves by decomposing to provide rich soil nutrients in which new trees grow. Seedlings growing around the base of trees are evidence of the good soil conditions.

Nature uses many different ways to decompose materials. Do certain types of decomposition only take place on certain types of trees? Hypothesize that regardless of the type of tree, more than one type of organism acts on it to decompose it.

Materials

- wooded area with decomposing logs on the ground
- hand-held garden tools (small shovel, pick)
- large-blade screwdriver
- hammer
- magnifying glass

Procedure

Locate a wooded area with many fallen trees that are showing signs of decomposing. Study several decomposing logs. Probe them with hand tools. Identify and record any organisms you find that are currently living inside the logs or evidence of their having been there. Some large organisms that might help break down a log are rodents, ants, carpenter bees (evidenced by perfectly drilled round holes in the wood), bracket (shelf) and other types of fungi, mushrooms, molds, mosses, worms, and insects in the larval stage (Fig. 5-3).

You do not need to identify the type of trees in order to reach a conclusion about your hypothesis. Simply record your findings on several logs, each having a different kind of bark.

Going Further

1. Use a tree identification book to identify the types of logs.

2. If you identify a particular type of fungi on a dead log, can you find a live standing tree where the fungi live too? Do the organisms that attack live standing trees continue to attack it when it is dead? Woodpeckers, for example, will nest in dead standing trees but not in trees that lie on the ground. This is because they generally make a nest habitat 8 to 10 feet above the ground. Do any other organisms use the fallen nest?

3. Measure the temperature inside a decaying log and inside a dead standing tree. If the temperature is higher in one, would you assume it is decomposing faster?

Fig. 5-3. *Identify the organisms that decompose trees.*

PROJECT 5-7
Making Gardens out of Ant Hills

Overview

Some animals produce waste materials that contribute to the richness of the soil around where they live. They might ingest soil along with other food, process it, and excrete it in a form that is beneficial to other life forms, such as plants. In this project, we will use soil from the mounds of ant hills and attempt to grow plants. Hypothesize that soil from the ant hill mounds contains more nutrients needed by plants, and that a plant grown in mound soil will be as healthy as a plant grown in local soil (which does not contain ant hills). Perhaps your hypothesis could be that the mound-soil grown plant will actually be better (be sure to qualify better—greener leaves, taller, etc.).

Materials

- fast growing seeds, such as green bean seeds
- soil from ant hills
- gravel or small stones
- soil from your area that is free from ant hills
- 2 small flower pots

Procedure

Pour about a half inch of gravel or small stones in the bottom of two flower pots. This acts as a drain to keep roots from becoming water logged. Fill one flower pot the rest of the way with local soil.

Locate a colony of ants outside (Fig. 5-4). Gather enough soil from the ant hill mounds to fill the other small flower pot.

Fig. 5-4. *Ant hills contain waste from ants.*

Plant several fast growing seeds, such as green bean seeds, in each pot. Place the pots in a sunny window. Water regularly using only tap water with no additional nutrients.

Make daily observations and record them in a log. Conclude whether your hypothesis was correct.

Going Further

1. Grow several plants in potting soil and several plants in ant hill soil. The larger sample size will make your results more meaningful.

2. Grow different types of plants and vegetables. Grow for a long period of time, until flowered plants bloom or vegetables mature.

3. Worms process soil through their digestive system. They remove anything they can use and excrete the rest into the soil. Run a similar experiment using soil from worm habitats.

6

Waste Products

We live in a "throw-away" society. Much of our food (meats, vegetables, desserts) come packaged in containers. Practically every household item comes in a box or wrapper, including items we use daily such as razors, diapers, cleaners and soaps, and hand towels. Some packaging (like blister packs, colorful boxes, and oversized packages) are not necessary but are used only for marketing purposes to entice people to buy the product. Not too many years ago, people would repair many of the items they owned. Ink refills were available for pens. Cigarette lighters were refillable with lighter fluid and flints. If a chair or toaster broke, it would be repaired. Today it would most likely be discarded and a new one purchased.

The manufacturers of some appliances plan them to be obsolete in a relatively short time. The purpose for "planned obsolescence" is to make people buy more products. The automobile industry has been accused of building cars that only last a few years before they begin to wear out.

Houses are sometimes knocked down instead of maintained and repaired. This is especially true in resort areas where the land on which one house stands could be used for a condominium dwelling housing three or four families instead of one. Some individuals move and "recycle" old homes.

We are overwhelmed with garbage and trash. Many communities are having difficulty dealing with the high cost of collecting, hauling, and disposing of trash. Throwing something in a trash can is not getting rid of it. It must be taken to a landfill and stored. "Biodegradable" products are products that decompose in a "reasonable" amount of time. A banana peel will decompose within a year, but a plastic bottle might take 1,000 years.

If we can't throw a product away, perhaps we should not be allowed to make it in the first place. Perhaps we should build things to last longer and repair them when they break down. What do we do with radioactive materials, such as U238, which is used to generate electricity? It must be stored for tens of thousands of years before it becomes safe.

These are questions that you as an individual and society must study, discuss, and possibly make life-style changes if we are to protect our environment.

PROJECT 6-1
Buried but Not Forgotten

Overview

A "biodegradable" material is one that is able to be broken down by the environment. It will decompose and return nutrients to the earth. Collect 20 items and hypothesize which will decompose quickly in the soil and which will not.

Materials

- 2, plastic, one-gallon milk jugs
- scissors
- shovel
- one- or two-foot square of soil (backyard)
- collection of 20 small items,
  10 of which you believe will decompose within
  a few months and 10 which you believe are not
  biodegradable, or at least that will not break
  down in a short time

Procedure

Collect 20 small items, 10 of which you believe will decompose quickly and 10 which will not. These items might include: a two-inch square piece of newspaper, a paper clip, a pencil, a penny, a rubber band, an old toothbrush, a two-inch square of clothing material, a piece of a breakfast cereal box.

Cut the top half off of two, one-gallon plastic milk jugs (use caution when working with sharp scissors). Carefully punch holes in the bottom and sides. These milk jugs will be used to hold the test items when they are buried. The holes will allow water to pass through the containers.

Place 10 objects in one of the milk containers that you hypothesize will begin to show signs of decomposition in three months. Using the chart shown in Fig. 6-1, identify the items placed in the container. Place 10 objects that you hypothesize will show no signs of decomposition in the other container. Record those items on the chart.

Dig two holes, each about a foot square. Place one container in each hole, and cover with soil. Wait three months.

Dig up each of your test samples, identify each sample and record how they look on the chart. Were any items totally decomposed to the point where you can't find them? Was your hypothesis correct?

Item #	Items hypothesized to begin decomposition		Items hypothesized to remain the same	
	Object name	Condition after 3 months	Object name	Condition after 3 months
1				
2				
3				
4				
5				
6				
7				
8				
9				
10				

Fig. 6-1. *Decomposition chart for* Buried but Not Forgotten *project.*

Going Further

1. Leave samples buried for longer periods of time, such as six months, or perhaps a year.

2. What organic materials can you add to the soil to increase decomposition? Try citrus fruits and their peels, which contain acid.

3. What organisms were present when you dug them up that might aid in decomposition? Larvae, worms? Identify them.

4. Did the grass over the buried container that had the most decomposition grow better than other spots in the lawn?

PROJECT 6-2
Plastic Graveyard

Overview

Plastics are among the most useful materials we use in modern society. They can be molded easily and have unique properties. Piano keys, food containers, doll babies, television cabinets, soda straws, squeeze spray bottles, model airplanes, hairbrushes, and thousands of other items we use daily are made out of plastics.

There are different kinds of plastics, phenolic, urea, melamine, cellulose, acrylic, vinyl, polyethylene, styrene, and many more. Each is chemically different.

Hypothesize that some plastics decompose more quickly than others. You might hypothesize instead that all plastics are bad for the environment because none of them will break down readily.

Materials

- 10 different plastic objects
- one-gallon plastic milk jug
- scissors
- shovel
- one-foot square area of soil
  (in your backyard)

Procedure

Collect different plastic objects, such as a hairbrush, ballpoint pen, piece of a kitchen trash bag, piece of a mouthwash bottle, piece of a milk container, and other similar items. Record each item on the chart shown in Fig. 6-2.

Carefully cut the top from a one-gallon plastic milk jug. Have an adult poke a few holes in the bottom of the container to allow water to pass through. Place the objects in the jug. Dig a small hole in the backyard and bury the container with the objects.

After three months, dig up the objects and evaluate them. Record your results on the chart. Was you hypothesis correct?

Going Further

1. Can plastics be made to decompose by adding something to the soil? Try burying citrus fruits and their peels, along with the plastics. This will introduce acid into the soil.

2. Is temperature or moisture a factor in decomposition?

Item #	Plastic object	Condition after being buried
1		
2		
3		
4		
5		
6		
7		
8		
9		
10		

Fig. 6-2. *Plastic decomposition chart for* Plastic Graveyard *project.*

PROJECT 6-3
Above or Below

Overview

Weather and other components in the air can cause decomposition. A good example of this is the rust that forms on metals that are left outside: swing sets, porch nails, lawn mowers, bicycles, etc. In the ground, micro-organisms, acids, and other components also act to decompose objects. Hypothesize which location decomposes fastest for 10 common objects, above ground or below ground. Should some objects be placed in a sanitary landfill that is exposed to the air and not covered?

Materials

- 10 different household objects
- shovel
- 2, one-gallon, plastic milk jugs
- one-foot square area of soil
  (in your backyard)
- one-yard square piece of screen
- few bricks or cinder blocks

Procedure

Collect two pennies, two hair pins, two pens, two pieces of newspaper, two rubber bands, and similar items commonly found around the home. Collect a total of 10 different items, two of each one.

Using scissors, carefully cut the top from two, one-gallon plastic milk jugs. Poke holes in the bottom. This will allow water to pass through. Place one of each item in each container. Record each item on the chart shown in Fig. 6-3. Bury one of the containers underground. Place the other container outdoors where it will be exposed to rain, sun, and other weather elements. Cover the container with a piece of screen held down by bricks, cinder blocks, or stakes. This will keep strong winds from blowing the test objects away. It will also keep cats and other nosy animals out.

After three months, dig up the buried items. Evaluate both the items above the ground and those that were buried. Record your results on the chart, and conclude whether your hypothesis was correct.

Going Further

1. Above ground landfills might attract birds. Do birds aid in the decomposition of landfill material? Do rats benefit the decomposition of landfill material?

2. Does sunlight and evaporation cause some materials to crack and decompose faster? Try rubber, leather, and cinder block.

Item #	Object name	Condition after being buried	Condition after being above ground
1			
2			
3			
4			
5			
6			
7			
8			
9			
10			

Fig. 6-3. *Above ground vs. below ground decomposition chart for* Above or Below *project.*

PROJECT 6-4
Preserving Our Goods

Overview

Materials that contain iron are decomposed by oxidation. This is the result of oxygen combining with iron to form rust. You have seen it on playground equipment and other outdoor objects made of metal. In this experiment, you will test several coating solutions. Hypothesize which solutions will offer the best protection against rust. This test will include samples both below the ground and above the ground.

Materials

- iron nails (do not use galvanized or other nails that are designed to prevent rust)
- 2 short lengths of wood (2 × 4 or something of similar size, about one or two feet long)
- hammer
- paint
- motor oil
- petroleum jelly
- shovel
- small plot of soil (in your backyard)

Procedure

Using a hammer, pound four nails equally spaced in one board (Fig. 6-4) and four nails equally spaced in another board. Paint one nail on each board with paint. Coat another nail on each board with motor oil (you can use a paintbrush, cotton swab, or an old rag). Coat a third pair of nails with petroleum jelly. The fourth nail on each board will be untreated and will be the "control" nail in the experiment. Use paint to identify each coated nail by painting a number on the board next to each nail.

Bury one board underground and leave the other above ground, exposed to the weather. After three months, evaluate all eight nails. Was your hypothesis correct or incorrect?

Going Further

1. Do the experiment for a longer period of time.

2. Weigh each nail before the test begins and again months later. Evaluate them for loss.

3. Aluminum does well in weather. How does it do buried in soil?

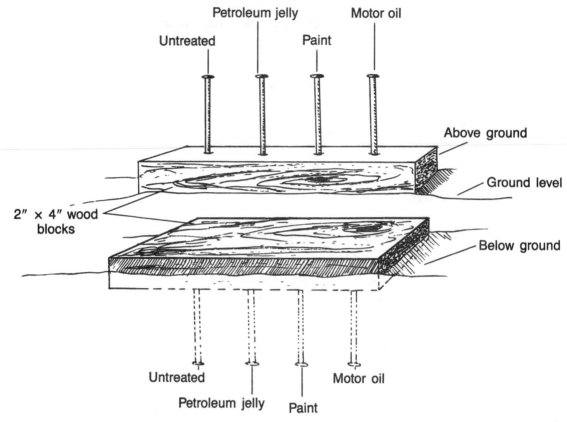

Fig. 6-4. *Testing nail coatings to prevent decomposition.*

PROJECT 6-5
Soak It Up
Adult Supervision Required

Overview

Wood structures often need to be in contact with the ground. Various outbuildings and landscaping schemes use wood that is partially buried in soil. In this experiment, you will hypothesize which soaking solutions offer the best preservation of buried wood. Be advised that this is a long-term project, which should take a year to get results.

Materials

- 4, 1" × 1" sticks of pine wood, each about 14 inches long
- 3, two-liter soda bottles
- scissors
- pint of linseed oil
- pint of paint
- pint of wood preservative
- marker or crayon
- one square foot of ground (backyard)
- handsaw

Procedures

Carefully cut four 1" × 1" sticks of wood to about 14 inches long or have an adult do it. Each stick should be the same type of wood. You should be able to buy some scrap, white pine wood at a local lumberyard.

Cut the top ⅓ off of three, two-liter, plastic soda bottles (exercise caution when using sharp scissors). These will be used as containers in which the wood will be treated with preservatives. Pour linseed oil in one container, paint in another, and wood preservative in another. Stand one stick upright in each container and let it soak for three days (Fig. 6-5). The fourth stick will be the control stick, and it will not be treated with anything. Using a marker, label each stick to identify how it was treated.

After soaking, push each stick into the ground to a depth that covers the treated area on the stick. For best results, leave the sticks undisturbed in the ground for six months to a year, then pull the sticks out of the ground and evaluate them. It takes a long time for decomposition to take place. Use your results to decide whether or not your hypothesis was correct.

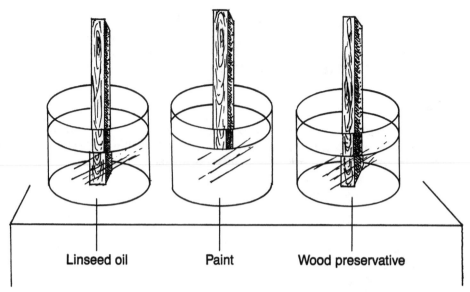

Fig. 6-5. *Testing different types of wood preservatives.*

Going Further

1. Perform the experiment using different liquid mixtures as preservatives (soaps, waxes, furniture polishes, turpentine).

2. A short-term project would involve soaking the sticks overnight, then cutting them in half to see how deep the preservative penetrated. Did any reach the center? Is it necessary to soak into the wood in order to preserve it, or will a thin coating be enough? Use different soaking times.

3. Wood must often come in contact with water, such as pilings for docks. Instead of burying the sticks in soil, submerge them in water for a period of time. Use water from a local bay, ocean, stream, or lake. Replenish the water as it evaporates.

4. Experiment with different types of wood: oak, pine, cedar, chestnut, hickory, and others.

PROJECT 6-6
Compact Campfire
Adult Supervision Required

Overview

People who have large trees on their property can often be seen in Autumn raking leaves, twigs, bark, and other natural tree litter from their front lawns. This collection is usually stuffed into plastic bags and hauled away by sanitation trucks (Fig. 6-6). Not only is the tree litter wasted, but plastic bags contribute to the refuse being thrown away.

Fig. 6-6. *Utilizing tree litter as fuel by making "litter bricks."*

A better use for dry leaves, twigs, bark, and other woody tree material might be as a fuel. Hypothesize that tree litter that would ordinarily be discarded as waste can be dried and compressed to form a "fuel brick," which could be used for fueling campfires and cookouts.

Materials

- collection of dry leaves, small twigs, bark, pine needles, pine cones, sawdust and other woody tree material
- trash bags or cardboard boxes to collect the tree material
- trash compactor
- outdoor barbecue pit

Procedure

Collect tree litter material as described in the materials list. Use cardboard boxes or trash bags to collect and store the materials.

Break the larger twigs into smaller pieces. Mix the materials together as best as possible to evenly distribute the leaves, twigs, and other litter.

Load a trash compactor with the tree litter mix. Compress it, add more litter, and compress it. Continue adding and compressing until the compactor is full.

Make several bricks using this method. Let the resulting fuel bricks dry in the hot sun for several days.

Have an adult light a campfire or a barbecue pit (parks often have barbecue pits constructed out of cinder blocks). Place one brick at a time in the fire. Record the length of time each produces usable heat energy. Conclude whether your hypothesis was correct.

Going Further

1. How can the combustion rate be reduced to make it burn longer? Will mixing bigger branch pieces in with small pieces help?

2. Fire logs are self-starting. Can we make our fuel bricks able to be ignited easily? Could it be constructed with a wooden log in the middle?

PROJECT 6-7
Soap Box Opera

Overview

Usually it is more economical to buy products in larger quantities. For example, a five-ounce box of brand X laundry detergent might cost $3. Dividing five into $3 gives us a cost of 60 cents per ounce. A 10-ounce box might cost only $5, making the cost per ounce 50 cents. Buying in bulk might also have more advantages than simply cost, however. We can lessen the impact on the environment if we create less waste products. The products we buy come packaged, wrapped, in a carton, a box, or some type of container. Every box needs a top and a bottom, regardless of how much of the product (be it soap powder, dish detergent, etc.) is inside. To package more of the product, perhaps only the container's sides need extending. Does this make the ratio of carton material to the quantity of product lower?

Hypothesize that buying in larger quantities also requires less carton (or other container) material to store it per unit measure of the product. If your project finds this to be true, then society could generate less waste by only selling products in bigger quantities.

Materials

- two-liter, plastic bottle of soda
- three-liter, plastic bottle of soda
  (same brand as above)
- small box of laundry detergent
- jumbo size box of laundry detergent
  (same brand as above)
- low count box of facial tissues
- high count box of facial tissues
  (same brand as above)
- small kitchen or postal scale

Procedure

Remove the caps and metal bands on the neck of the two-liter and three-liter soda bottles. Weigh each empty container that will be tested: the two- and three-liter bottles, the small and large box of laundry detergent, and the low and high count box of facial tissues.

Divide the weight of each empty container by the amount of product. For example, divide the weight of a two-liter bottle of soda by 2. Divide the weight of a three-liter bottle by 3. Divide the weight of a small empty box of laundry detergent by the number of ounces in it. FIll in the chart shown in Figure 6-7 with these numbers.

Product name	Weight of empty container	Quantity of product material	Ratio of product to container
2-liter soda bottle			
3-liter soda bottle			
Small laundry detergent			
Large laundry detergent			
Low count facial tissues			
High count facial tissues			

Fig. 6-7. *Chart for comparing product container sizes to the amount of product stored for* Soap Box Opera *project.*

Evaluate the data you have collected and determine whether or not your hypothesis is correct.

Going Further

1. Organize a consumer awareness group and suggest the removal of one- or two-liter bottles if your hypothesis is correct. If your hypothesis is incorrect, perhaps suggesting the removal of three-liter bottles should be considered. Who would be contacted?

2. Compare container size to shelf life. A large amount of product might not be efficient for a small family if the product spoils before it is all used.

7

Indoor Environment

When the word environment comes up in conversation, the great outdoors immediately comes to most people's mind. But the environment really refers to wherever you (or any other organism) might find itself. We ourselves, as human beings, are an environment for many living microscopic organisms. They live on and in us.

People find themselves in many different daily enclosed environments: home, car, plane, bus, school, work place, elevator, restaurant, office, and even a tent. We require many things from our environment. We need air, a certain range of temperatures, light, food, and drinking water. Love and creative challenge are among other needs that are less easily quantified.

Because we find ourselves indoors much of the time, indoor environments are very important. Some uncomfortable conditions can be tolerated for a short time: a crowded elevator, a smoke-filled room, noise from machines in a factory, a cold draft blowing in from a window that someone else wants open, a loud radio when you are trying to study. We can put up with the close proximity of other people squeezing into an elevator because we know we will only be there for a minute or two. Projects dealing with indoor environments measure conditions that affect our mental and physical health.

PROJECT 7-1
My Walls Are Weeping

Overview

Relative humidity is a measure of the amount of moisture in the air. Humans have a humidity range in which they feel most comfortable. A room with an airtight woodstove burning might make the air unusually dry. People's lips become chapped and their skin dry. Dry air is also unhealthy. Spores become airborne when they are dry, thus increasing chances for allergy attacks. Small, closed areas, such a bathroom might become too humid when someone takes a hot shower. The high moisture content makes it difficult to dry off. As water condenses on various objects, it might encourage the growth of molds. Water droplets can drip to the floor causing a stain on rugs or even rotting wood. The jacket on a toilet tank is one of the first places you will notice water droplets forming. The cold water in the tank condenses water vapor in the moist warm air as it comes in contact with the tank surface. Cold water pipes in the bathroom, basement, and other areas may "sweat" on hot, humid days. Hypothesize which areas of the house are the most humid most often.

Materials

- hygrometer or sling psychrometer
- thermometer
- pad and pencil

Procedure

Draw a chart such as the one shown in Fig. 7-1. Write down a list of rooms and other areas in the home. Measure the temperature and humidity (amount of moisture in the air) at each location. Use a hygrometer or a sling psychrometer to measure humidity. Record this data. Also make note of any observations. Do pipes have condensation on them? Is their mildew around toilet tanks or shower curtains? Is mold present around the refrigerator door seal?

Study your data and conclude whether or not your hypothesis was correct.

Going Further

1. At what temperature in each room does condensation occur (sort of an "indoor dew point").

2. Commercial cleaners can be purchased at supermarkets to remove molds. Can anything be used to help prevent molds from forming in areas where warm, moist air encourages mold growth?

Location in home	Temperature	Humidity	Observations
Bathroom before shower			
Bathroom after shower			
Kitchen			
Bedroom			
Attic			
Basement			

Fig. 7-1. *Indoor humidity chart for* My Walls Are Weeping *project.*

PROJECT 7-2
Air Garbage

Overview

Tiny pieces of material that float in the air are called "particulate matter." These very tiny particles can be dust, pollen, mold spores, lint, cooking grease and oils, and animal hair. Some particles are too small to be trapped by filters such as a vacuum cleaner bag. Hypothesize that a vacuum cleaner does not trap all of the particles that it sucks up. If this proves to be true, then people should vacuum their home *before* they dust the furniture, because the vacuum will actually take some particles from the rug and thrown them into the air.

Materials

- vacuum cleaner
- cellophane tape

Procedure

Stick two long strips of cellophane tape along the side of a vacuum cleaner bag (Fig. 7-2). Either an upright or a round canister type vacuum can be used. Take one strip off. Examine it to see if any particles of paper from the vacuum bag came off. If it did, we know that we will expect to see those particles on the test strip when our experiment is done, and we will not count those particles as part of the experiment.

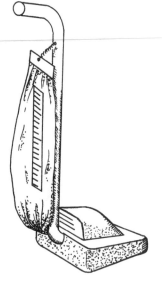

Fig.7-2. *Use transparent tape to collect dirt your vacuum cleaner lets escape.*

Run the vacuum cleaner over all the rugs in your home. When done, carefully remove the test strip of tape, and examine it. Can you detect the presence of any particles that travelled through the bag? Place the tape against a white sheet of paper to make any trapped particles more easily observed. Was your hypothesis correct?

Going Further

1. Will different tape locations on the bag vary the results? Is there a difference if the tape is placed on the inside bag instead of the outside bag?

2. Put a piece of filter paper or a coffee filter across the end of a dryer vent. Run the dryer. Did your filter trap particles that the dryer's filter didn't catch?

PROJECT 7-3
Dusting the Air
Adult Supervision Required

Overview

Even though we don't normally see particles in the air, the air is full of tiny pieces of lint, dust, pollen, mold spores, and animal hair (called "particulate matter"). We see these particles when they accumulate on our furniture or appear as dust balls and cob webs in the corner of a room. Hypothesize that some rooms have more airborne particulate matter than others. Your hypothesis might also name the rooms that you believe have the most (or least) amount of particulate matter.

Materials

- portable, electric fan
  (preferably one with a low speed setting)
- several wooden tongue depressors
- paper towel
- dish detergent
- moist sponge
- several plastic sandwich storage bags

Procedure

Thoroughly clean the blades of a portable electric fan. **Be sure the fan is unplugged from the wall whenever you work with the fan's blades**. Use a little dish detergent and a moist sponge with a paper towel to scrub the blades clean.

Place the fan in the living room and run it for one week. If there are small children in the house, be sure to place the fan at a location where they will not come in contact with it. At the end of a week, turn the fan off and pull the plug from the electric outlet. Using a tongue depressor, scrape all the particles you can from one fan blade. Place the stick along with the collected particles in a plastic sandwich bag and seal it. Label it as to which room the particles were collected from.

Clean the fan blades using soap and water. Place the fan in another room, such as in a kitchen. Run it for a week and again scrape the particles from one fan blade. Place it in a bag and label it.

Repeat this procedure for several rooms in your home, as suggested in the chart in Fig. 7-3. Did any room have more "dirt" than another? Were there any differences observed among the collected samples (you might want to use a magnifying glass to examine closely)? For example, was there more grease present in the samples collected from the kitchen than from the living room? Conclude whether your hypothesis was correct.

Location in home	Particulate Matter Collected	
	Quantity	Observations
Bathroom		
Living room		
Kitchen		
Bedroom		
Garage		
Basement		

Fig. 7-3. *Chart for collecting airborne particulate matter for* Dusting the Air *project.*

Going Further

1. Oil floats on water. Remove a filter from a vent that is above the burners on a stove in a kitchen. Fill a kitchen sink with water. Place the filter in the water. Does a layer of oil and trapped particles float to the surface of the water? What happens if you add a few drops of dish detergent to the vent or to the water?

2. There are areas in the house that are not easily accessed for every day cleaning. Check these areas for molds and pollen. Examples are molding around window frame tops, refrigerator grading, air conditioners, and heating vents.

PROJECT 7-4

No Noise Is Good Noise

Overview

There are times when people enjoy loud sounds, such as a Fourth of July fireworks display or a live music concert by their favorite performer. But for the most part, people need peace and quiet, especially when they are trying to relax or to study.

Hypothesize that thick shrubs planted around a home can help insulate it from the loud sounds of highway traffic, acting as a natural sound barrier.

Materials

- row of shrubs
- portable tape player and a song tape
- portable tape recorder with a VU meter on it or a sound level meter (such as Radio Shack's decibel meter 33-2050)
- yardstick

Procedure

Locate a line of shrubs. Place a portable tape player on one side of the side of the shrubs and play a tape with a song on it (Fig. 7-4). The volume should be turned up very loud. Stand on the other side of the shrubs and measure the sound by using a decibel meter. If you do not have a decibel meter, you could use a tape recorder that has a VU meter (sound level meter) on it. Observe the average sound level and the loud peaks in the music. Measure the distance between you and the tape player, or sound source.

Next, place the tape player at the same distance from you as you just did, but this time do it in a clear area where there are no shrubs or other obstructions between you and the player. Play the same selection. Measure the sound level. Was your hypothesis correct?

Going Further

1. Do the experiment on a very dry day and again on a day when the humidity is extremely high. Compare the results.

2. Using an audio oscillator, does the shrub barrier reduce sound at one frequency more than another?

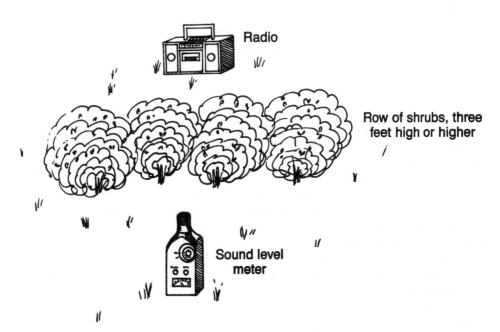

Radio

Row of shrubs, three
feet high or higher

Sound level
meter

Fig. 7-4. *Testing shrubs as natural sound barriers.*

PROJECT 7-5
Lead into Hot Water

Overview

It has long been known that heavy metals like lead interfere with the formation of red blood cells in the body. Heavy metals also cause brain deterioration. In the ancient days of the Roman Empire, many people died from lead poisoning, because the aqueducts that they carried their water in were made with lead.

By studying bones, archaeologists have determined this to be the cause of death. Baby cribs and window sill paints once contained lead. Some children chewed on these and now lead-based paints are no longer used for interior surfaces.

Often, lead-based paint is used to decorate pottery made in countries such as Mexico. Hypothesize that it might be possible that lead is being introduced into your family's food by eating and drinking from dinnerware containing lead and a lead test should be performed in every home to protect family members.

Materials

- chipped, ceramic tea cup
- lead test kit
  (available from some of the mail
  order supply
  houses listed in the Resource List)

Procedure

Gather a chipped, ceramic tea cup or coffee cup. The cup should be chipped or cracked, otherwise the glazing would prevent any lead in the ceramic from entering the food. Fill it with water. Let it sit overnight. If lead is present, it might migrate into the water. Using a lead test kit, test the water for any appreciable amounts of lead. Conclude whether your hypothesis was correct.

Going Further

1. Would a tea cup filled with tea, which contains tannic acid, cause more lead to migrate from the walls of the cup than would a tea cup filled only with water? How about other acidic beverages, such as orange juice and apple cider?

2. Test for aluminum contamination from aluminum utensils, cookware, and foil-wrapped foods.

3. Test for the presence of residual soap after you or your dishwasher has rinsed the dishes. Ingesting soap causes upset stomachs.

PROJECT 7-6
No Smoking Area
Adult Supervision Required

Overview

It is commonly known that cigarette smoking is hazardous to a persons health. In an enclosed space, such as a room or office, cigarette smoke can build up and endanger nonsmokers in the room. Naturally, the smoker receives the greatest amount of smoke and the particulate matter that is in smoke. Hypothesize that we can visually detect that an appreciable amount of smoke with each puff remains inside the smoker.

Materials

- adult cigarette smoker
- clean hankerchief
- unfiltered cigarette holder

Procedure

Hold a clean piece of a handkerchief between a cigarette holder and a cigarette. Have an adult smoker inhale two puffs. He should not exhale through the handkerchief.

Next, have the smoker inhale a puff of smoke directly from the cigarette and exhale through the cigarette holder with a clean section of handkerchief being held on the other end. Have him do this for two puffs. The purpose of using the cigarette holder in this experiment is to concentrate the smoke onto equal areas of the handkerchief.

Compare the color of the inhaled section of handkerchief to that of the exhaled section. Which is darker? Was some smoke left inside the person who smoked?

Going Further

1. Using the smoker, evaluate different filtered brands of cigarettes and non-filtered cigarettes. Cut up many two-inch squares of handkerchief, sheet, or other white material for the test so they can be easily mounted for display.

2. Compare cigarettes to pipes and cigars.

PROJECT 7-7
The Nose Knows
Adult Supervision Required

Overview

Most people don't think of odor as a form of air pollution. But imagine trying to eat dinner while the unpleasant smell of decomposing garbage fills the air. Odors that occur outdoors dissipate, that is, they spread out over a greater area and become less concentrated. But indoor odors stay around. Odor is as individual as taste. An odor that bothers some people might not be offensive to someone else. Many people find certain perfumes attractive while others can't stand the smell of them.

Supermarkets and department stores sell many different brands of room deodorizers, each claiming to make a room smell better. Nature provides us with a lot of plants and trees that smell fresh and appealing to many people. Rose petals, lilac petals, pine sap, cedar, and cinnamon are just a few aromas that most people find pleasing. Hypothesize that fragrances from natural substances can be as effective as commercially purchased deodorizers.

Materials

- onion
- 2 cardboard boxes of equal size and shape
  (about two feet long by one foot wide and one foot high)
- commercially purchased solid room deodorizer stick
- 4 saucers or small shallow dishes
- lilac or rose petals
- transparent tape
- utility knife (requires adult supervision when in use)
- kitchen knife
- several people

Procedure

Gather the items listed in the materials list above. You can use petals from either type of flowers, lilac or rose, whichever is more readily available to you.

Using a utility knife, have an adult cut a small flap about three inches square in one end of each box. The flap will be opened to permit smelling inside the box. It must be closed when not in use. A small piece of adhesive tape can be used to seal it shut.

Have an adult cut an onion in half. Place each half on a tea cup saucer with the open facing upward. Open the top of each cardboard box. Place one onion and saucer in the far, left corner in each box. This should be at the opposite end of the side with the sniff flap.

Place a solid commercial air freshener stick on a saucer and place it in the far right-hand corner of one of the boxes.

Crush the petals of several lilac (or rose) blossoms. Place them on a saucer and put the saucer in the far right-hand corner of the remaining box.

Close the top of both boxes. Using adhesive tape, seal the top of each box. After several hours, open the flap in the first box and sniff. Close the flap. Breathe some fresh air outside to clear your nostrils. Open the flap on the second box and sniff. Did the flower blossoms mask the onion smell as well (or better than) the commercial air freshener? Use several people and ask them which box had the strongest onion smell. Was your hypothesis correct?

Going Further

1. Do some types of smells work better covering specific odors? For example, if you were to snap open several pine twigs and place them in your box, would the twigs cover onion odor better than rose petals?

2. Experiment with placing various natural materials (pine needles, cedar bark, cinnamon, apples) in boiling water to release fragrances.

3. Experiment with man-made products that were not designed to be air fresheners, such as bubble gum, scented soaps, candles, spearmint breath mints.

8

Man Affects the Environment

Mankind is the only living thing on Earth with the ability to affect our planet on a massive scale. He can help save endangered animals by relocating them or saving their environment. He can turn a desert area into lush green oasis by building wells with irrigation systems and planting vegetation. He can also cause destruction, both on a small and large scale.

Human activities can affect the Earth's climate by changing properties of the Earth's surface, such a reflectivity, heat capacity and conductivity, the availability of water, dust and particulate matter, and aerodynamic roughness (smooth and rough ground affect wind turbulence in the area). Industrial factories can release particles in the air that can affect the temperature of the Earth. Some chemicals that mankind has invented can harm the environment. Chlorofluorocarbons, a chemical used in aerosol cans and air conditioners, is thought to be damaging the Earth's ozone layer, which protects the Earth from dangerous ultraviolet light. Oil spills from "tankers" kill wildlife and ruin seashore habitats. Sewage dumped into lakes (releasing nitrates) can create algae blooms, which contaminate drinking water.

This chapter contains project ideas dealing with mankind and the environment. Some projects will be concerned with how humans help the environment; others will be about harming it.

PROJECT 8-1
Outdoor Air Conditioning

Overview

Changing the natural reflectivity of the Earth's surface can affect the temperature of an area. People have constructed roads and driveways out of asphalt, where there was once grass, fields, or stands of trees. Hypothesize that, because objects that are black in color absorb more light, the air temperature near the ground will be warmer over an asphalt roadway than over a grass-covered lawn.

Materials

- thermometer
- half-gallon milk carton
- scissors
- 2 paper clips
- grass-covered lawn
- asphalt driveway
- sunny, warm day

Procedure

You need to measure the air temperature above the surface of a blacktop driveway and above a lawn. Locate a relatively large lawn near an asphalt driveway. The two should be near each other, say within a city block, because after you get temperature readings from one, you will have to quickly get temperatures from the other while the overall temperature and weather at that time of day remains the same. Both areas should be in direct sunlight and the day of the test should be warm or hot.

Construct a box such as the one shown in Fig. 8-1. You need to measure the air temperature over each test surface, so you need to build a small container that will let air flow freely through it but that will keep the thermometer out of direct sunlight. Cut flaps in all four sides as shown, and bend them open to allow air to flow through the carton. Open the top of a half-gallon milk carton so that it opens square. Uncoil a paper clip and wrap one end around the thermometer. Make a hook out of the other end. Hang the paper clip on the top of the carton and close the top, using the other paper clip to hold it shut. The thermometer will be suspended inside the milk carton. This construction is similar to professional weather stations, where instruments are contained inside wooden boxes that have vents, or louvers, in the sides. If you want to give the milk carton more strength, glue a wooden dowel in each corner.

Set the measuring device on a large lawn area. After about five minutes, read and record the temperature. As quickly as possible, place the

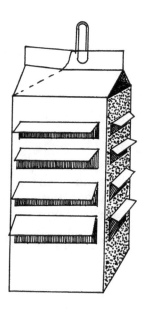

Fig. 8-1. *Construct a thermometer housing to measure the effect of colored surfaces on air temperature.*

thermometer on an asphalt driveway. After about five minutes, read and record the temperature. Compare the two temperatures and conclude whether your hypothesis was correct.

Going Further

1. Measure temperature differences on different surfaces, such as gravel or sand at a playground. Sand at a beach might be hard to test because a large body of ocean or lake water might interfere with temperatures in the area, usually lowering them.

2. Repeat the experiment on a cloudy day or in two shady areas.

PROJECT 8-2
Particular Particulates

Overview

The term "particulate matter" refers to very tiny pieces or "particles" of matter. Clap two chalkboard erasers together and you will see a cloud of particulate matter. In large quantities, airborne particles can block sunlight in the sky. Some particles in the air are released naturally, from volcanos or by sandstorms, for instance. Many activities of man result in airborne particulate matter. Wood-burning stoves, industrial emissions from smoke stacks, even automobile exhaust.

Particles in the air are not only unhealthy, but by blocking sunlight and preventing it from reaching the surface of the Earth, we might be changing the overall temperature of the Earth.

Hypothesize that the presence of particulate matter in the air will affect the amount of light, as well as the temperature, on the other side of a particulate cloud. Scientists agree that airborne particulate matter reflects sunlight as it tries to reach the Earth's surface, but they disagree on the long-term effect this will have. Some believe that the lack of sunlight could make the Earth cool down and cause another ice age. Some believe that the particulate matter could trap heat in the lower atmosphere and cause a "greenhouse effect." Either scenario is grim.

In this project, you will try to measure the amount of light blocked by particulate matter in the air and how it affects the temperature.

Materials

- slide or movie projector
- thermometer
- photo light meter (a device that measures the amount of light, usually in lumens, and is used by camera and photography people)
- flour
- flour sifter
- paper and pen

Procedure

Set a slide or movie projector on a table top. Several feet away, place a photo light meter pointing it at the light coming from the projector lens. Place a thermometer by the light meter (Fig. 8-2). Measure and record the temperature and the amount of light.

Fill the flour sifter full of flour. Briskly sift the flour, causing the fine particles of flour to fall between the projectors light source and the photo light meter. Measure and record the amount of light.

Fig. 8-2. *Testing air particulate matter and temperature.*

It will be hard to measure any reduction in temperature because you cannot be expected to sift very long. To find out what the temperature would be, you can simply move the light meter further away from the projector until you reach a point where the level of light without looking through sifted flour is the same as it was at the beginning point when the air was full of particulate matter. Place the thermometer at this point and read the temperature. Was your test equipment accurate enough to detect any difference in light or temperature in this experiment? Conclude whether your hypothesis was correct.

Going Further

Rainwater has a pH, which is a measure of acidity or alkalinity. Air contains sulfur dioxide, which increases the acidity and lowers the pH. Measure the pH of rain at the beginning of a rainstorm and again at the end. Will the early rainwater have a lower pH (higher acidity) than rainwater gathered four or five hours later? Will the air actually be scrubbed clean by the raindrops?

PROJECT 8-3
Every Litter Bit Burns

Overview

The forest floor is covered with fallen trees, branches, twigs, leaves, evergreen needles, and other natural materials. These materials are called litter. The litter accumulates over the years. A big problem for forests is uncontrolled fire. In some states, controlled burning is used to burn off the litter to prevent it's accumulation. Controlled burning is a technique used by forest fire fighters to prevent uncontrollable fires from destroying a forest. If litter is allowed to increase and a fire occurs, the litter acts as fuel, which burns very hot and sets trees on fire. If, on the other hand, the litter is burned off every two or three years, there is not enough fuel to set the trees on fire. Therefore, a fire will be easy to control and cause little or no loss of trees.

It is natural for some fires in nature to be beneficial. Forests can be cleaned out and fertilized. The seeds of some trees are only released by forest fires. The Jack Pine (pinus banksiana) requires a temperature of 140 degrees Fahrenheit to open the cone and the seed to come out. Nevertheless, uncontrolled fires can cause too much damage to wildlife, forests, and property loss, and should be contained.

Often, the litter that is control-burned is along the side of roads where accidental fires are likely to start from careless campers or cigarette smokers.

Will litter on the forest floor capture and hold moisture? If so, how much? Can this moisture help reduce the advent of forest fires? Will litter from hardwood trees be more flammable than from softwood trees? Hypothesize which type of litter holds moisture better, litter from hardwood trees or from softwood trees. Hardwood trees are trees whose wood is more dense. These include oak, hickory, and chestnut. Pines, balsa, and firs are examples of softwoods.

Materials

- bucket and shovel
- scale
- forest area in a stand of hardwood trees
- forest area in a stand of softwood trees
- ruler
- 2 pieces of screen, about two-foot square
- several bricks or other heavy objects

Procedure

The day after a heavy rain, locate a stand of hardwood trees and a stand of softwood trees in a forest. Using an undisturbed forest area in a stand of hardwood trees, remove a one foot by one foot area of litter (small twigs, leaves, and tree "stuff") that covers the soil. Similarly, in a stand of softwood trees, remove a one foot by one foot area of litter that covers the soil. Weigh each sample and record the results on the chart in Fig. 8-3.

	Hardwood litter sample	Softwood litter sample
Wet weight		
Dry weight		
Moisture content (wet-dry)		
Percent of moisture to the whole sample		

Fig. 8-3. *Measuring moisture content of hard vs. soft wood tree litter chart for* Every Litter Bit Burns *project.*

Lay each sample outside in a dry sunny spot for three or four days. Place a piece of screen over each sample to prevent any material from blowing away. Use bricks or other heavy weighted objects to hold the screen in place. Keep the screen loose and not pressing down on the litter samples so that air can freely circulate through it.

After the samples have dried, weigh them again and record their weight. Subtract the dry weight from the wet weight for both samples and record the results on the chart. This calculated weight is the amount of moisture that was held in the sample.

$$\frac{\begin{array}{r}\text{hardwood wet weight}\\ -\text{hardwood dry weight}\end{array}}{\text{weight of moisture}} \qquad \frac{\begin{array}{r}\text{softwood wet weight}\\ -\text{softwood dry weight}\end{array}}{\text{weight of moisture}}$$

Next, divide the moisture weight by the original wet weight and multiply by 100 to get the percent of moisture in each sample.

$$\frac{\text{weight of moisture}}{\text{wet weight}} \times 100 = \text{percent of moisture held}$$

For example, if a soil sample weighed three pounds when it was wet and two pounds when it was dry, then:

$$3 - 2 = 1$$
$$1 \div 3 \times 100 = 33\%$$

The sample material with the larger percent figure is the sample that holds the most moisture. Was your hypothesis correct or incorrect?

Going Further

Measure flammablity **(adult supervision required)**. Are softwoods more flammable, making them more susceptible to forest fires. Dip dried pine needles in water and dried leaves in water. Try to set fire to them. Which one burns easier?

PROJECT 8-4
Clean Up Your Act

Overview

Water that has become contaminated can often be filtered to clean it up. Consider an aquarium tank. The water is not changed very often. Instead, it is constantly filtered through a filter medium, such as activated charcoal and angel hair. In an aquarium setup, activated charcoal filters soak up some of the undesirable chemicals in the water. They also trap minute dirt particles. Filters using angel hair remove large particles and also provide a home for certain bacteria, which cause chemicals in the water to be less toxic to the fish.

Water can travel faster through some filtering materials than others. If a material is more dense, water will travel slower through it, but perhaps the water is more thoroughly cleaned. Hypothesize that filter materials that filter faster will not clean the water as well.

Materials

- food coloring
- activated charcoal (available at pet shops)
- angel hair (available at pet shops)
- sand (that has been rinsed clean)
- several coffee filters
- 5 test tubes
- test tube rack or stand that can hold five test tubes in a row
- funnel
- ring stand
- water
- kitchen measuring cup with pouring spout
- spoon
- masking tape and pen
- cheesecloth
- wristwatch with a second hand (or a stopwatch)
- white sheet of paper

Procedure

Place four test tubes in a test tube rack. Set a funnel on a ring stand and position it so that the test tube rack can be slid into position underneath the funnel to catch filtered water in the desired test tube. Stick a piece of masking tape on each test tube, numbering them 1 through 4, to indicate what each test tube will hold. Fill the kitchen measuring cup with water. Add four drops of dark food coloring (red, blue, or green) to the water and stir.

Some of the filter material you will be testing requires a screen to keep it from falling through the hole in the funnel. A piece of cheesecloth (for strength), together with a paper coffee filter (to hold tiny particles), should contain all filtering material. These will not contribute to filtering out any of the color in the water. Nevertheless, to make the experiment valid, place a lining of cheesecloth and paper coffee filter at the bottom of the funnel for each filter material that is being tested, even if the material does not need it to be held in place in the funnel.

Some of the test material might need to be rinsed so that it does not add any color of its own to the results. Run clear water through the setup to flush it. Let it dry before performing experiments.

Line the funnel with the cheesecloth and the coffee filter. Pour activated charcoal into the funnel. Position a test tube under the funnel. You will use the fourth test tube as a measuring device during the experiment as a control for color comparison later. By filling the fourth test tube with the colored water, you will know how much to pour into the funnel without overflowing the receiving test tube. Fill the measuring test tube with colored water. Pour it into the funnel. Catch the filtered water in test tube #1. Use a stopwatch or the second hand on a wristwatch to determine the amount of time it takes to drain all of the water through the filter. Use the chart in Fig. 8-4 to record your data.

Test tube number	Filter medium	Drain time in seconds	How does it compare-color
#1	activated carbon		
#2	angel hair		
#3	sand		
#4	control-colored water with no filtering		
#5	control-plain clear tap water		

Fig. 8-4. *Chart for recording media filter project data for* Clean Up Your Act *project.*

Remove the filter paper, cheesecloth, and activated charcoal from the funnel. Rinse the funnel clean. Line the funnel with a fresh piece of cheese cloth and a fresh paper filter. Fill the funnel with angel hair. Slide the test tube rack to position the second test tube under the funnel. Again, using the extra test tube for measuring, pour colored water through the filter setup. Record the time it takes to drain through.

Repeat the procedure a third time using sand as the filtering material. Be careful not to splash any filtering water into the other test tubes to prevent contaminating those samples.

You should now have three test tubes filled with filtered water. Fill the fourth test tube, which we have been using for measuring, with the colored water. Place it in the test tube rack. This will be the control tube, where no filtering has taken place. Add a fifth test tube that contains only plain tap water and no coloring. Compare the color of each sample and record your observations on the chart. Place a white sheet of paper or cardboard behind all of the tubes to aid your observations.

Examine the drain times and the color of the filtered samples to reach a conclusion about your hypothesis. Which material provided the best filtration at an acceptable speed?

Going Further

1. Use other materials as filters (potash, soil, cotton).

2. Perform the same experiment but use plastic sandwich bags full of filtered watered solutions instead of test tubes. Shine a light through each bag and use a photo light meter to record the amount of light passing through each. A small rope and two clothespins could be used to suspend each bag. The light meter gives a number in lumens, thus making evaluation quantitative rather than observational. Be sure to control the distances.

PROJECT 8-5
Flying Fly Ash

Overview

Very tiny particles called particulate matter come from many sources and can become airborne, causing air pollution. Some smoke from the chimneys of factories and even home woodburning stoves and fireplaces can send particulate matter into the air. Hypothesize that smoke from chimneys or smoke stacks contribute measurable amounts of particles to the air. Because some people live in the city and some in rural areas, this project is given in two versions.

Materials

- microscope
- plastic food wrap
- 8 glass microscope slides
- clear adhesive tape
- access to someone's property who has a working fireplace or woodstove (city dweller's do not need this item)
- knowledge of the current wind direction (from local television, radio, wind sock, or home wind indicator)

Procedure

Rural residents: Locate a chimney where the ground around it is accessible. If you have a home, a woodburning stove or fireplace will work best. This project could be done using a factory but it is usually hard to get near a factory. You would have to get permission from anyone whose property you are on. We will assume this project is centered around your home chimney.

Take a piece of clear adhesive tape, such as Scotch™ tape, and tape it to itself making a loop. Turn it inside out so the sticky side is on the outside. Stick it to a glass microscope slide. Prepare eight slides in this same manner.

Set up eight "stations" at equal distances from the chimney in a pattern that covers north, northeast, east, southeast, and so on. Each station consists of a glass slide with sticky tape on it to collect airborne particles.

For several hours while the fireplace is in operation (have an adult tend the fireplace), expose the collection stations. Make note of the wind direction. This can be done by watching your local weather on television or listening to a radio, using a home wind indicator, or setting up a wind sock. Be sure the wind does not dramatically switch directions during the hours of collection. The wind velocity must be five miles per hour or less.

After several hours of collection, place pieces of plastic food wrap over the samples to prevent contamination. If your hypothesis is correct, the samples that are downwind of the chimney will capture more particles than those in other directions. Use a microscope to study the particles you have collected. Was your hypothesis correct?

City residents can do this project another way. Using microscope slides with sticky tape on them, place one on the side of a building downwind of an industrial smokestack. Place another slide on the opposite side of the building. Does the slide exposed to the prevailing wind from the factory show more particles than the other? Was your hypothesis correct?

Going Further

1. Does particulate matter come in stronger concentrations on one side of your house than on the others? If so, don't open the windows on that side.

2. When pollen is in the air during pollen season, does it accumulate on one side of the house more than the others?

PROJECT 8-6
Oil and Water Don't Mix
Adult Supervision Required

Overview

There is an old saying "Oil and water don't mix." Indeed, this is true. Oil is lighter in weight than water so it floats on top. Floating petroleum and other products cause much environmental damage each year. Hypothesize that man's pleasure boating activities contribute to water pollution.

Materials

- cotton swabs, such as Q-tips™
- 2, plastic, gallon milk jug containers
- body of water and dock where boaters fuel up
- magnifying glass

Procedure

Fill two, plastic, gallon milk jugs with only enough water so that they float in the water at a depth where the caps just break the surface.

Locate a body of water used by pleasure boats such as a back bay or lake. At a clear spot in the water, perhaps by a fishing pier, carefully lower one milk jug. Let it float for a few minutes. Slowly lift the jug out of the water. As you pull up, capillary action will cause any petroleum film to adhere to the outside of the bottle. Using a cotton swab, wipe a three-inch square area from the side of the jug.

Find an area in the water near a dock where boats fuel up (Fig. 8-5). As was done previously, dip the second jug into the water. Slowly lift it out to collect any surface petroleum products. Use a cotton swab and wipe the same size area as was done on the last jug.

Using a magnifying glass, examine the material collected on the two cotton swabs. Was your hypothesis correct or incorrect?

Fig. 8-5. Oil and oil products commonly used by boats float on the surface of the water.

PROJECT 8-7
Group Rates

Overview

In the early days of our country, most people lived very close to where they worked. Today, it is just the opposite. Most people must use some sort of vehicle transportation to get to work. With so many people on the move, mass transportation in populated areas frequently exists in the form of buses, trains, trolleys, and other shuttle vehicles. There are other advantages to using public transportation too. In places like New York City, it might cost as much to house your car as it does to house your family. Also, too many vehicles on the road cause pollution and traffic congestion.

Hypothesize that mass transportation saves the nation's fuel and reduces pollution by moving more people for a given supply of fuel.

Materials

- access to a bus company or bus driver
- access to an adult driver with a car
- access to the operator of another mode of transportation (optional)

Procedure

Research the average fuel cost to run a bus. A bus company might provide you with this information. You could ask a school bus driver to calculate the miles per gallon the bus gets on average. To determine a vehicle's miles per gallon, follow these steps:

1. Fill the bus with gasoline. Record the reading on the odometer. This is the starting mileage figure.

2. After driving until the tank gets low (maybe several days), record the number of gallons needed to fill the tank. This number is shown on the gas pump.

3. Subtract the starting mileage figure from the current odometer reading. That gives the miles traveled.

4. Divide the miles traveled by the gallons used. The result is the vehicle's fuel efficiency expressed in miles per gallon.

5. Divide the miles per gallon for the mass transit vehicle by the number of people riding (including the driver). This will give the miles per gallon per person.

Conclude whether your hypothesis was correct.

Going Further

1. Compare other modes of transportation and the mileage they get on a gallon of gas. Is there a local trolley, tram, subway, or train? In Tokyo, Japan, many people use bicycles to get around.

2. Set the whole project up as a computer program.

3. Ask the Environmental Protection Agency for emissions data on buses, cars (4, 6, and 8 cylinders). Include diesel-fueled vehicles too. Compare the amount of exhaust emissions to the number of people the vehicle can carry.

Resources List

This resource list is compiled to give you a mail-order source for science supplies.

Carolina Biological Supply Company
2700 York Road
Burlington, NC 27215
800-547-1733

Edmund Scientific Company
101 E. Gloucester Pike
Barrington, NJ 08007
609-573-6250
Free catalog available

Fisher Scientific
4901 W. LeMoyne St.
Chicago, IL 60651
1-800-621-4769

Frey Scientific Company
905 Hickory Lane
Mansfield, OH 44905
1-800-225-FREY

Science Kit & Boreal Laboratories

777 East Park Drive
Tonawanda, NY 14150-6782
800-828-7777

Sargent-Welch Scientific Company

7300 North Linder Ave.
PO Box 1026
Skokie, IL 60077
312-677-0600

Heath Company

Benton Harbor, MI 49022

Sells electronic equipment, weather instruments, computers, and test equipment.

Glossary

aerobic decay—the breaking down of a material by microorganisms in the presence of oxygen.

anaerobic decay—the breaking down of a material by microorganisms in the absence of oxygen.

biodegradable—products that can be broken down naturally by the environment (decompose) within a reasonable amount of time.

biome—a classification of an area by the conditions that exist in that area. Biomes have specific climates, deserts are hot and dry, rain forests are wet and humid, the polar caps are dry and cold.

carnivorous plants—animals- and insect-eating plants, such as Venus's-flytraps, sun dews, and pitcher plants.

climate—the long-term weather average of a large geographic area.

companion planting—growing different plants together to benefit one or both plants. Bush beans and potatoes planted in alternate rows help both plants. The beans keep Colorado potato beetles out of the potatoes and the potatoes keep Mexican bean beetles out of the beans.

control group—When doing experiments, a control group is the group that has all of the variables maintained. For example, if you want to test for effects of carbon monoxide on plants, you must have two equally healthy plants. Both plants will receive exactly the same care and conditions (soil, sunlight, water) and one plant, the experimental plant, will receive additional carbon monoxide. The other plant is the control plant. The control plant is maintained while the experimental plant receives the variation.

decomposition—the breaking down of a material by the elements and by microorganisms.

dew point—the temperature at which moist air must be cooled for saturation to occur. If the temperature is below freezing, the dew point is sometimes called the frost point.

ecology—the relationship of organisms to other organisms and to their nonliving environment. Ecology deals with habitat, food chains, and life cycles.

environment—the surroundings where you (or an organism) find yourself—outdoors, home, plane, car, school, bus, restaurant, tent, and so on.

erosion—the wearing away of a material. Erosion can be caused by friction, water, ice, wind, sand, chemicals, and temperature extremes.

experiment—a planned way to test a hypothesis.

gestation period—the time it takes a female organism to carry a developing baby until it is born.

humus—a mixture of decomposing organic material that returns nutrients to the soil.

hypothesis—an assumption—based on influence from scientific data—made prior to testing for a conclusion.

insectivorous plants—plants that eat insects, such as the Venus flytrap, sun dew, and the pitcher plant. Some plants eat animals as well as insects. They are called "carnivorous" plants.

leech—to run water through slowly and dissolve out nutrients.

minerals—naturally occurring, inorganic material (they are not alive nor do they come from living things), made up of one or more elements (like silicon, oxygen, iron). Combinations of minerals make up rocks.

nocturnal—animals that sleep in the day and become active at night.

observation—looking carefully.

particulate material—tiny pieces of material that float in the air, composed of particles of dust, pollen, mold, spores, lint from fabrics, cooking grease and oils, and animal hair.

pest—someone or something that is a nuisance or that causes trouble. A garden pest could be a rabbit that eats the vegetables which the gardener is trying to grow.

predator—animals that prey on other animals.

116

quantify—to measure.

relative humidity—the percentage of moisture the air is holding.

sample size—the number of items under test. The larger the sample size, the more significant the results. Using only two plants to test a hypothesis that sugar added to water results in better growth would not yield a lot of confidence in the results. One plant might grow better simply because some plants just grow better than others.

scientific method—a step-by-step logical process or investigation. A problem is stated, a hypothesis is formed, and an experiment is set up, data is gathered, and a conclusion is reached about the hypothesis based on the data gathered.

tree litter—decomposing parts of a tree that have fallen from the tree and cover the ground—leaves, twigs, needles, seeds, pieces of bark.

weather—the daily changes in the local atmosphere, caused by moving air and gases, tiny particles, and water vapor (wind, rain, snow, fog).

weed—an undesirable or unwanted plant growing among other plants. A rose growing in a barley field is a weed, even though roses are prized flowers.

About the Authors

Robert Bonnet holds an MA degree in environmental education, and has been teaching science at the junior high school level in Dennisville, New Jersey for more than 15 years. He is also a State Naturalist at Belleplain State Forest in New Jersey. During the last seven years, he has organized and judged many science fairs at both the local and regional levels. Mr. Bonnet is currently the chairman of the Science Curriculum Committee for the Dennisville school system and a science fellow at Glassboro State College.

Dan Keen holds an Associate in Science Degree, majoring in electronic technology. Mr. Keen is a computer consultant who has written many articles for computer magazines and trade journals since 1979. He is the coauthor of two books published by TAB Books, *Mastering the Tandy 2000* and *Assembly Language Programming For The TRS-80 Model 16*. In 1986 and 1987, he taught computer science at Stockton State College in New Jersey. His consulting work includes writing software for small businesses and teaching adult education classes on computers.

Together, Mr. Bonnet and Mr. Keen have had articles published on a variety of science topics.

Index

decay (cont.)
  natural vs. man-made substances
    (plastics), 59
  odors produced by, 94
  oxygen (oxidation) and rust, 75
  plastics, 71
  recycled vs. "new" paper, 56
  temperature vs. rate of, 61
  weather exposure to increase, 73
  wood, 26, 62
  wood preservatives vs., 77
deodorizers, natural products for, 94
dramatic presentation, 5
drought, 6
dust, 86, 88, 100, 108

E_____

earthworms, 65
ecological projects, 21-35
  decomposition of wood, 26, 62
  fat (blubber) as insulation, 30
  food supply vs. populations, 32
  footprints to identify animals, 35
  gestation periods vs. life spans, 24
  habitat size vs. number of
    organisms, 22
  habitat size vs. size of animals, 23
  hair and fur as insulation, 28
  sugar water feeder, 35
  water attracts animals, 35
ecosystems, 7
environmental science, 5-6
  balanced systems, 6
  closed systems, 6
  interaction of organisms, 6
  man's impact on environment, 6
  natural "disasters," 6
experimentation, 1, 3

F_____

fat, insulation value of, 30
fertilizers, 11, 54, 60, 64
filtering water, 105
fires, 6, 102
flammability, 104
floods, 6
fly ash, 108
food chains, 21
forest fires, 6, 102
fuels
  conservation of, 111
  leaves as, 79

fungi, 62, 84
fur, insulation value of, 28

G_____

gestation periods, life spans vs., 24
greenhouse effect, 100
habitats, 21
  size of vs. number of organisms in,
    22
  size of vs. size of organisms in, 23
hair, insulation value of, 28
herbicides
  black walnut tree produces, 50
  natural substances as, 47, 50
hibernation, 17
humidity
  noise vs., 90
  relative humidity, 84
humus, 8, 15
  bacteria and oxygen to produce,
    60, 73
  biodegradable trash as, 54
hygrometers, 84
hypothesis, 1, 2, 3, 5

I _____

ice ages, 100
illustrations, 5
indoor environment, 83-95
  cigarette smoke, 93
  dust in air, 86, 88
  lead pollution in hot water, 92
  noise pollution, 90
  odors and air pollution, 94
  oil suspended in air, 89
  relative humidity, 84
information gathering, 1, 5
insectivorous plants, 11
insects
  ants, attractors and repellents for,
    39
  ants, soil nutrients in ant hills, 64
  attracting, 38
  color to attract or repel, 41
  decay caused by, 62
  marigolds as repellent for, 42
  nocturnal, light vs. heat attraction,
    40
  spiders, webs, prey, 48
insulation
  fat as, 30
  hair and fur as, 28

J_____

judging science fairs, 4-5

L_____

lakes and ponds (see also water)
  percolation of water through
    bottom of, 12
  temperature of soil on bottom, 17
lead pollution, 92
life cycles, 21
  gestation periods vs. life spans, 24

M_____

man's impact on environment, 6,
    97-112
  acid rain, 101
  filtering water, 105
  fly ash, 108
  forest fires: good or bad?, 102
  greenhouse effect: dust in air, 100
  oil spills, 110
  particulate matter in air, 100, 108
  reflective surfaces vs.
    temperatures, 98
  transportation and pollution, 111
measurements, 2
models, 3
molds, 62, 84, 86
mosses, 62

N_____

natural disasters, 6
nitrogen, testing topsoil for, 11, 27,
    64
noise pollution, 90

O_____

observations, 5
odors, 94
oil spills, 97, 110
organic matter (see humus)
oxidation, protection from, 75
ozone layer, 97

P_____

particulate matter, 100, 108
  dust in home, 86, 88